THE WESTMINSTER SOURCE BOOKS
FOR MINISTERS

THE CHRISTIAN SACRAMENTS

THE WESTMINSTER SOURCE BOOKS
FOR MINISTERS

The Funeral . . . . *by Andrew W. Blackwood*

The Christian Sacraments . . *by Hugh Thomson Kerr*

(*Other volumes in preparation*)

THE
CHRISTIAN
SACRAMENTS

A Source Book for Ministers

HUGH THOMSON KERR

PHILADELPHIA

THE WESTMINSTER PRESS

To My Two Preacher Sons
Hugh Thomson Kerr, Jr., Ph.D.
Donald Craig Kerr, Th.D.

Foreword

ACCORDING to Calvin's very simple but comprehensive statement two things make a Church: the faithful preaching
of the Gospel and the faithful administration of the sacraments. Perhaps it is not too much to say that the Protestant
Churches, on the whole, have regarded preaching as of pre-
eminent importance and have obscured the place of the sacraments. On the other hand, the Roman and Greek Churches,
and that group in the Episcopal and Anglican Churches that
leans toward the Roman ritual, have unduly exalted the sacraments and have neglected the ministry of the Word. The true
doctrine of the Church demands that the presentation of the
Gospel should be by both Word and sacrament. The Lord's
Supper, in the words of Emil Brunner, is not magic but an
"illustrated Word of God." The sacrament does what the
Word of God does. It is given "in order that we might not
merely hear the message of divine grace but also see it and perceive it more clearly." [1]

It is encouraging to note that there is renewed interest in
the place and efficacy of the sacraments. This is due to several
reasons. There is, first of all, a new emphasis upon the value
of the Christian Church. While the Church is an organiza-
tion, an institution of world significance, it is seen to be essentially a corporate fellowship, a society of believers, through
which the Spirit of God ministers to the souls of men. The
old cynicism that condescended to recognize the Church but
with reluctance has given place to the definite acknowledgment of its central mission in the world. We no longer hear
the question, What is wrong with the Church? but everywhere
we find appreciation of the meaning and significance of the
Church as the divine *koinonia* where the rich are poor and the
poor are rich, where the weak are strong and the strong are
weak, and where Christ is all and in all. This revival of the

7

place and position of the Church has added new significance to the sacramental element in faith and worship.

There is, also, a heartening release from the rationalism of a past generation and a return to faith in the superrational. There is a recognition that the ultimate mystery in life is bound up with the question how spirit is related to the body, the unseen to the seen, the heavenly to the earthly, the spiritual to the material, the divine to the human. This will always remain in the realm of mystery, but it need not be a mystery that partakes of the irrational. It has been said that we do not know how the spirit of the sculptor gets into his statue, or the spirit of the painter into his picture, or the spirit of the musician into his song, or the spirit of the architect into his building, but we do know that it does; and in like manner we do not know how the Spirit of Christ ministers through the sacrament of baptism, or through the sacrament of the Lord's Supper, but we know that he does, and for those who worthily receive the same, they become in very truth " the viaticum of our earthly journey." The experience of the Church is that the Holy Spirit ministers through the sacraments, even as through the Word. There is no doubt that the neglect of the sacraments has brought about the impoverishment of evangelical Christianity. There has been on the part of many of the clergy no consistent interpretation of the sacraments, and too often they have been administered in such a way that their efficacy has been obscured. The Roman doctrine can be expressed and interpreted. The Zwinglian position can be readily explained, but the Reformed doctrine is not easy to comprehend. There is, however, urgent need that the place of the sacraments be more fully recognized in Christian worship, for, as Karl Barth has said, " with regard to the Sacrament the Evangelical Church has made a grave mistake. There is undoubtedly a connection between the neglect of the Sacrament and Protestantism's becoming Modernist. Certainly the sermon is the proper cultus-act, but it ought never to have been isolated in the way this happened in the Evangelical Church.

As the seal is the reminder of the action of the King, and as
such indispensable, so the Sacrament (not in the Roman Catholic sense) must come again into its own. It should be obligatory for the Holy Communion to be celebrated at every service, which is, as is well known, what Calvin strove for." And
he adds: " The Roman Catholic Church has a sacramental service without preaching. . . . We have a service with a sermon
but without sacraments. Both types of service are impossible." [2]

The importance of the sacraments in the life and worship
of the Christian Church is evident from the fact that when
the Church began the sacraments began. Principal John S.
Whale has said: " These rites of Baptism and Eucharist go back
to Christ himself. There is nothing older than this in Christendom. Before theology; before all our ecclesiasticism; before even a word of the New Testament was written this was.
This is the earliest Gospel." [3] It is for the purpose of focusing
attention upon the efficacy of the sacraments in Christian life
and worship that this book is written. It seeks to set the sacraments in their proper place in the Christian tradition and also
endeavors to interpret them from the New Testament point
of view. The book does not aim to travel the difficult path of
critical scholarship. That path has been traced in countless
volumes of sacramental controversy. While presenting positions in accord with scholarship, the book seeks also to outline
methods by which the active pastor may enrich his ministry
and the service of the Church through the proper and more
frequent administration of these sacred ordinances. If what
has been written draws attention to teaching long obscured,
and to customs and traditions rooted in the history of the
Christian faith, the author's purpose will be fulfilled.

HUGH THOMSON KERR.

Shadyside Presbyterian Church,
Pittsburgh, Pennsylvania,
1944.

Acknowledgments

ACKNOWLEDGMENT for permission to use material quoted in this book is made to the following:

American Baptist Publication Society
    Straton, *Baptists: Their Message and Mission*
E. P. Dutton & Co., Inc.
    Everyman's Library, *Christmas Books*, by Dickens
    Major, Manson, and Wright, *The Mission and Message of Jesus*
Harper & Brothers
    Coffin, *What to Preach*
    Sweet, *Religion on the American Frontier, The Presbyterians*
Houghton Mifflin Company
    Lowell, " The Vision of Sir Launfal "
P. J. Kenedy & Sons
    Gasparri, *The Catholic Catechism*
Longmans, Green & Co.
    Lowrie, *The Lord's Supper and the Liturgy*
The Macmillan Company
    Hadfield, *Psychology of Power*
    Masefield, " The Everlasting Mercy "
    Brilioth, *Eucharistic Faith and Practice, Evangelical and Catholic*
    Klausner, *From Jesus to Paul*
    Hoskyns, *Cambridge Sermons*
    Jeans, *The Mysterious Universe*
The Methodist Publishing House
    The Discipline of the Methodist Church

John Murray
    Jowett, *Epistles of St. Paul*
Oliver & Boyd, Ltd.
    Maxwell, *Genevan Service Book*
Oxford University Press
    Bowman, *A Sacramental Universe*
    Milligan, *The Ministry of Worship*
The Provincial Elders' Conference of the Moravian Church
  in America
    Moravian Hymnbook and Liturgy
G. P. Putnam's Sons
    Stephens, *The Child and Religion*
Saint Anthony Guild Press
    Marucchi, *Manual of Christian Archeology*
Charles Scribner's Sons
    Brunner, *Our Faith*
    Ibsen, *Emperor and Galilean*
    Bushnell, *Christian Nurture*
Mrs. Harry Webb Farrington
    Harry Webb Farrington, " His Living Presence "

Contents

I. Our Sacramental World

THE Christian sacraments belong to the Christian revelation. They were instituted by Christ and practiced in the Early Church before the Gospels or the Epistles were written and before the Church was organized. Together with the preaching of the Gospel they were the first expressions of Christian community life. In this sense they hold a primary place in Christian worship. Immediately after Pentecost the early Christians were baptized into the name of the Lord Jesus and "day by day, continuing stedfastly with one accord in the temple, and breaking bread at home, they took their food with gladness and singleness of heart." [1] The immediacy of the sacraments is an arresting fact.

The sacraments, however, like the Incarnation, are related to the things of sense and to the world about us. Even as the Word of God was made flesh, so the mystery of the sacraments is related to the world of sense. God uses natural mediums to make available spiritual values. This is possible because all nature is, in a sense, symbolic. The things that are seen speak to the soul of man of things that are not seen. When, therefore, we speak of the sacraments as being symbols and signs, we are saying nothing that goes beyond the general revelation of God's active presence in the world. The whole world is symbolic, "so that what is seen hath not been made out of things which appear." [2]

It has been said that there is a day view and a night view of the world. The day view gives us a world that is alive with intelligence and spiritual purpose. It is the world which is the garment of spirit, the abode of the living God and of the children of God made in his image. The night view gives us a world which is wholly physical, material, and without meaning. The day view shows us a universe in which the purposes of the living God are at work. The night view gives us a uni-

verse which is all mechanism. It is the day view that makes
the world the abiding place of spirit and gives it spiritual significance. There has been, of course, an age-old struggle, both
in religion and philosophy, between the day view and the night
view. The day view is not confined to Christian thinking, for
philosophers in all ages and of all races have set forth the truth
that there is a numinous world, as well as a world of sense.

The late Professor Archibald Allan Bowman, of the University of Glasgow, before his lamented death, gave to the
world the substance of his teaching in a volume entitled *A Sacramental Universe*. It was his contention that the world is
something other than it seems. It has value and meaning.
Things that are substantial possess spiritual significance.
"There are," he says, "numberless possibilities of being for
which the purely physical is not accountable. The rich and
varied manifold of the sensible, which we see around us, is the
composite product of the physical and the spiritual. Take
spirit out of the world, and ' nature ' disappears, leaving only
a barren waste of undulating ether waves, for ever in motion,
breaking out here and dying down there, reinforcing one another and obliterating one another by the process known to
the physicist as interference." [3] This world is both spiritual
and physical, and it is this fact that makes possible the revelation of God in and through the sacraments.

This point of view is familiar, but its implications are not
always clear. We can lay hold of the world with our eyes and
ears and hands, but there is always something lying beyond
our grasp which eludes us. The universe, we feel, is the garment of the unseen. It is the embodiment of the invisible, the
manifestation of the spiritual, the expression of a Spirit who
hides himself within his own creation. In other words, the
world is alive, not dead. Like the wayward traveler of old, we
think we are alone in the night, with only the darkening heavens for a canopy and a stone for a pillow, when suddenly we
find ourselves in God's great cathedral, surrounded by heavenly companions, visitants from the invisible, and in the silence

we hear the voice of the Eternal saying, " I am with thee." It is in this sort of world our lot is cast — a world in which the things that are seen conceal, and at the same time reveal, another world of spiritual reality.

The Bible, of course, is the great champion of what Professor Bowman calls " a sacramental universe." Paul gave expression to this conception in simple and concise language: " The invisible things of him since the creation of the world are clearly seen, being perceived through the things that are made, even his everlasting power and divinity." [4] The Old Testament repeats the thought that the visible is but the garment of the invisible. What magnificent symbolism is contained in its pages: " Have ye not known? have ye not heard? hath it not been told you from the beginning? have ye not understood from the foundations of the earth? It is he that sitteth above the circle of the earth, and the inhabitants thereof are as grasshoppers; that stretcheth out the heavens as a curtain, and spreadeth them out as a tent to dwell in; that bringeth princes to nothing; that maketh the judges of the earth as vanity. Yea, they have not been planted; yea they have not been sown; yea, their stock hath not taken root in the earth: moreover he bloweth upon them, and they wither, and the whirlwind taketh them away as stubble. To whom then will ye liken me, that I should be equal to him? saith the Holy One. Lift up your eyes on high, and see who hath created these, that bringeth out their host by number; he calleth them all by name; by the greatness of his might, and for that he is strong in power, not one is lacking." [5] Indeed it is impossible to escape from the ever-pursuing Presence.

> " If I ascend up into heaven, thou art there:
> If I make my bed in Sheol, behold, thou art there.
> If I take the wings of the morning,
> And dwell in the uttermost parts of the sea;
> Even there shall thy hand lead me." [6]

We remember how Shackleton and his two companions, in their lonely trek across the ice lands of the Antarctic, when with

every step they faced death, afterward confessed to each other
that they were conscious of a fourth but unseen companion
who kept step with them. It is something not to explain but
to experience. The Scripture always and everywhere bases its
message upon the reality of the unseen. "The things which
are seen are temporal; but the things which are not seen are
eternal." [7]

We are introduced to the same interpretation of the world
by many scientists who today have cast aside the "night view"
of the universe. The teaching that "man is destined to ex-
tinction in the vast death of the solar system" has given place
to a spiritual interpretation of the universe. To many modern
physicists it is not spirit that is mysterious; it is matter, for
matter, as it is called, breaks down under the pressure of scien-
tific analysis and leaves us with something invisible. The scien-
tist no longer measures things he sees with the foot rule of the
engineer, but with the "golden reed" brought to him in the
hands "of an angel." [8] "Today," says Professor Jeans, "there
is a wide measure of agreement, which on the physical side of
science approaches almost to unanimity, that the stream of
knowledge is heading toward a non-mechanical reality; the
universe begins to look more like a great thought than like a
great machine. Mind no longer appears as an accidental in-
truder into the realm of matter; we are beginning to suspect
that we ought rather to hail it as the creator and governor of
the realm of matter — not of course our individual minds,
but the mind in which the atoms out of which our individual
minds have grown, exist as thought. . . . We discover that the
universe shows evidence of a designing or controlling power that
has something in common with our own individual minds." [9]
To us the universe begins to look more like *a great thought*
than like a great machine. Behind what looks like a machine
there is an inspiring intelligence. Always and everywhere
in our mysterious universe "the unknown transcends the
what we know." [10] It is true, of course, that the physicist, as
physicist, never escapes from the measurable, for the unseen

with which he deals is still within the universe. Nevertheless, the implication of his teaching is that there is something beyond, which he terms "invisibility," and he feels justified in asserting that what lies beyond is "the finger of God agitating the ether."

This, also, is the philosophy of the poet. He sees beyond the things other men see. Francis Thompson saw Jacob's ladder and the angels of God, not at Beth-el, but at Charing Cross, and beheld Christ walking upon the waters, "not of Gennesareth, but Thames." When the eyes of Saul Kane were opened he saw, not the scenery with which he was familiar in his unregenerate condition, but an entirely new world:

> " O glory of the lighted mind.
> How dead I'd been, how dumb, how blind.
> The station brook, to my new eyes,
> Was babbling out of Paradise;
> The waters rushing from the rain
> Were singing Christ has risen again.
> I thought all earthly creatures knelt
> From rapture of the joy I felt." [11]

That was a spiritual awakening which enabled a man who had been a beast to see in the station brook the river of Paradise, and to hear the swirl of the waters singing of Easter morning. In like manner there is the spiritual genius of William Blake, who saw a treeful of angels at Peckham Rye, watched the sun rise over the horizon of the world, and instead of seeing color heard the heavenly choir singing, " Holy, Holy, Holy! " All true literature has this power of vision, and the writings that endure contain meanings too deep for words. The books that live on through the centuries are those that see beyond the visible: the works of Homer and Dante, Shakespeare, and *Alice's Adventures in Wonderland, A Christmas Carol,* and the Mother Goose rhymes. In his introduction to *A Christmas Carol,* Chesterton says: "Many writers, for instance, have called the gold and chrysolite of the Holy City a vulgar lump of jewellery. But when these critics themselves attempt to

describe their conceptions of future happiness, it is always some
priggish nonsense about ' planes,' about ' cycles of fulfilment,'
or ' spirals of spiritual evolution.' Now a cycle is just as much
a physical metaphor as a flower of Eden; a spiral is just as much
a physical metaphor as a precious stone. But, after all, a garden is a beautiful thing; whereas this is by no means necessarily
true of a cycle, as can be seen in the case of a bicycle. A jewel,
after all, is a beautiful thing; but this is not necessarily so of a
spiral, as can be seen in the case of a corkscrew. Nothing is
gained by dropping the old material metaphors, which did hint
at heavenly beauty, and adopting other material metaphors
which do not even give a hint of earthly beauty." [12] It is language " which did hint at heavenly beauty " that opens our
eyes to see what we should otherwise have missed. Instead of
believing in two or seven sacraments the poet lays hold of only
one, for the whole universe becomes for him symbolic. To
Francis of Assisi for whom all nature was vocal, there was
cause for joy because of all created things: " our brother, the
Sun," " our sister, the Moon," " our brother, the Wind . . .
and all weather," " our mother, Earth," " our brother, Fire,"
" our sister, Death." Everything, to Saint Francis, signifies
to us God.

The sacraments, however, go beyond the language of words.
The symbolism of words fails us, and we resort to other forms
of expression. Robert Browning has a few verses, which he
calls " One Word More," in which he tells us in what varying
ways he sought to express his love. Poetry failed him. Art
failed him. Music failed him. He vainly sought some other
form of expression through which he might make manifest
his heart's desire.

> " This I say of me, but think of you, Love!
> This to you — yourself my moon of poets!
> Ah, but that's the world's side, there's the wonder,
> Thus they see you, praise you, think they know you!
> There, in turn I stand with them and praise you —
> Out of my own self, I dare to phrase it.

> But the best is when I glide from out them,
> Cross a step or two of dubious twilight,
> Come out on the other side, the novel
> Silent silver lights and darks undreamed of,
> Where I hush and bless myself with silence." [13]

Even silence speaks where words fail, and we resort to art, to music, to some form of sign language, to symbolism in action. Words fail because there are other things in life than things intellectual. Ideas do not make up the whole of life, and symbols, while sometimes substituting for words, move on into a world where words fail. Language has never been able to express all that the simple symbol of the cross means to the Christian. For this reason the use of religious symbols has been world-wide. The swastika, for example, far from being an Aryan symbol is found in almost every land both of the Orient and the Occident. The symbol of the tree of life has age-old history. The more mystical and indefinable a religion is, the more luxuriant is its symbolism. Mystical Hinduism has more of symbolism than matter-of-fact Mohammedanism. The Hindu has laid under tribute all that he has found in the universe to express what to him is the unknowable. His religion is replete with symbols that speak to him concerning the secret of life. In like manner, the Jewish and Semitic religions are rich in symbolism. We open the Old Testament and immediately we are introduced to the Garden of Eden and the ritual of sacrifice. In the furnishings of the tabernacle we have a wealth of symbolism that bewilders us: the seven-branched candlestick, the ram's horn, the ear of corn, the palm branch, the cords and curtains with their distinctive coloring. The Temple itself was a symbol and everything in it symbolic: the Holy of Holies, the Ark of the Covenant, the shewbread. The Old Testament writers frequently left language for symbolism: the basket of summer fruit, the blossoming almond tree, the valley of dry bones, the serpent of brass, the taking off of the shoe, the peace offering, the sin offering, the scapegoat, the incense, the long hair of the Nazirite,

the Sabbath, the numbers three and four and seven with their
hidden meanings.

It would be strange if the Christian religion, the most spiritual of all world faiths, did not make use of symbolism.
When we open the New Testament we come face to face with
the ritual of baptism and the ordinance of the Lord's Supper,
symbolizing a changed mind and a redeemed life. The Church
itself began with the Pentecostal symbolism of the " sound as
of the rushing of a mighty wind " and the appearance of
" tongues parting asunder, like as of fire." [14] Our Lord himself
resorted to the symbolic again and again. It was this language
he used when he washed his disciples' feet, when he rode upon
the colt in his triumphant entry into Jerusalem, when he broke
the bread and fed the assembled multitude " with five barley
loaves, and two fishes," when he changed the water into wine,
when he spoke of the baptism wherewith he himself was to be
baptized. To John every miracle of Jesus was a sign, and
those miracles which he selected to have a place in his Gospel
are chosen signs of the work of God in the hearts of men.

In making known his will for his followers, Christ chose
to appoint certain symbols, and gave to them such significance
that they are not merely symbols of spiritual realities but sacramental symbols. John Calvin defined a sacrament as " an
outward sign, by which the Lord seals in our consciences the
promises of his good-will towards us, to support the weakness
of our faith." [15] The sacraments are indeed " outward signs,"
and many Christians never advance beyond this interpretation. Indeed they are satisfied with it. The sacraments to
them are outward symbols of an inner spiritual grace. The
water of baptism suggests to them cleansing from sin and
purity of life. If they adhere to the mode of baptism by immersion, it is a symbol of death unto sin, and resurrection unto
newness of life. The Lord's Supper, in like manner, is a symbol. The bread and the wine represent our Lord's broken body
and shed blood. He alone is the Bread of Life, the Water of
Life, and these symbols speak to the believer. By faith we

feed upon him. In partaking of them, by faith we partake of him.

This is the accepted interpretation of many Christians and it satisfies them, but it stops short of what is meant by a sacrament, and the question, " When does a symbol become a sacrament? " awakens century-old controversies. It is customary to say that the sacraments are not only symbols and signs but seals. The action involved moves beyond the symbolic. " In the sacraments the visible symbols provide an objective epitome of Christ and His benefits of such a kind as to seal assurance about them on our hearts." [16] In the sacraments something is done. Assurance is given; promises are vindicated; the Gospel is proclaimed; Christ is present. " The essential thing in the Sacraments is not what we say and do in them but what God in Christ says and does in them." [17]

The sacraments are indeed symbols and become the divine language by which God conveys his revelation. Yet they are not symbols in any natural or narrow sense, but are symbols that are also seals. Through them " Christ and the benefits of the new covenant " are conveyed to " believers." [18] The language is carefully chosen. Even as Christ is present in the Word, so he is present in the sacraments. God takes of the things of sense, using them as signs and symbols of things spiritual and invisible, and through them conveys Christ to the believer. The sacramental world can suggest, but cannot give us a sacrament in this Christian sense. The Christian sacraments come to us from the hand of Christ. He institutes the sacraments and, like the Word of God, they become for us the divine revelation and vehicle of his grace.

It is here that we step up out of the natural into the spiritual, out of the seen into the unseen, out of sensible signs into sacramental values. The sacraments become for us not only symbols but *seals*. A seal is a substitute for a signature. It authenticates the transaction. When Jezebel wrote letters in the king's name she " sealed them with his seal." The seal gave to the documents royal authority. It is a word frequently found in the writings of Paul and taken no doubt from the ratification of the Covenant. Writing to the Romans he discusses the meaning and significance of the rite of circumcision. It was both a sign and a seal. Abraham, he says, " received the sign of circumcision, a *seal* of the righteousness of the faith which he had while he was in uncircumcision: that he might be the father of all them that believe." [19] Commenting upon this language, Matthew Brown Riddle says: " The true idea of a Sacrament is here suggested: it is a sign, seal, and means of grace, but not grace itself. Circumcision is not the Covenant: nor is baptism regeneration. The sign and seal is not itself the ground of confidence, but it testifies and openly ratifies a Divine covenant or blessing. If Abraham needed a seal of the righteousness reckoned to him, some such outward sign and seal may be expected in the Christian church." [20] The sacrament is God's seal vindicating, ratifying, authenticating the covenant of grace to Christian believers.

We are physical beings, living in a material universe, encompassed about by the things of sense, yet conscious of a " presence that disturbs " us " with the joy of elevated thoughts "; and through the things of sense, the things we see and handle, God by his Holy Spirit ministers to us of his grace. He may speak to us through the glory of the sunset and the murmur of the wind, but in the sacrament, through the water, through the bread and the wine, which are the symbols of spiritual realities, he " seals " to us " Christ and the benefits of the new covenant." Through the indwelling and blessing of the Holy Spirit the things of sense become sacramental. The sacramental value is, however, not in the symbolism, not in the water " set apart," not in the bread or the wine consecrated upon the holy table, not in the words of the institution, not in the person who administers the sacraments, but in the complete sacramental act, which is one and through which the Holy Spirit, and he alone, seals to believing recipients the blessings of the new covenant.

In the words of the Old Scots Catechism, " It hath the verity joined with it," for without the accompanying work of the Holy Spirit the sacraments, whatever be the mode of their administration, must be only an empty form. Calvin placed the emphasis where it must always be placed. " I assign this office," he says, " to the sacraments; not from an opinion of their possessing a perpetual inherent virtue, efficacious of it-self to the advancement or confirmation of faith; but because they have been instituted by the Lord for the express purpose of promoting its establishment and augmentation. But they only perform their office aright when they are accompanied by the Spirit." [21]

The sacraments belong to both earth and heaven. Water and bread and wine are of this world, but, since this is a sacra-mental world, they can signify that which they are not. Sir Edward Burne-Jones, in speaking of the genius of Michel-angelo, said, " There's a lump of pigment at the end of his brush and by the time it has been laid on the stucco there is something there that all men with eyes can recognize as divine." The master had taken pigment and brush and canvas, and had used such earthly things to manifest the divine. In a much higher sense, Christ takes of the things of earth and causes them to signify the things of heaven. By his Spirit the sacra-ments become seals, authenticating, verifying, and confirm-ing his own words and promises. In the sacrament he is active. It would seem, says Professor MacLeod, " as if religious experi-ence were a kind of collision, sometimes a violent collision. We know God, so to speak, only when God pleases to hit us." [22] In this odd expression the thought is suggested that it is God who, in religious experience, is actively at work. He causes something to happen. So in the sacraments, where religious experience is at its best, God the Father, God the Son, God the Holy Spirit, is actively present. The sacrament, like the Word, is a " given thing."

II. The Christian Sacraments

GOD makes use of common things to manifest his grace to men. The supreme example of the divine condescension is the Incarnation. Our Lord Jesus Christ " existing in the form of God, counted not the being on an equality with God a thing to be grasped, but emptied himself, taking the form of a servant, being made in the likeness of men." [1] Flesh and blood became the vehicle of him who was Very God of Very God. In this miracle of the Incarnation the divine and the human became eternally wedded, and, henceforth, manifestations of God's grace and glory in lesser degree may be expected. If nature can become the means through which the supreme manifestation of God becomes possible, it will not be difficult for us to accept his use of the things of sense to convey grace to men. Indeed there have been those who have contended that the sacraments are but the extension of the Incarnation, but such language goes beyond the revelation given us. Nevertheless, the same principle which makes the Incarnation possible also furnishes a rationale for the sacraments. The sacramental idea is bound up with the spiritual interpretation of the universe.

It is not surprising, therefore, that there have been those who maintain that everything in life is sacramental and that there have been groups of Christians who have set aside the sacraments and counted their celebration unnecessary. The Society of Friends, popularly known as the Quakers, has no sacraments; yet among them we find Christians of deep piety and high spiritual perception. The Edinburgh Conference on Faith and Order, in its studied discussions concerning the sacraments, was sincerely perplexed as to how to formulate a basis of Church fellowship that would include the Friends, but reached no conclusion. What fellowship in sacramental worship can there be between Friends and sacrament-observing Christians?   To the Friends, Christianity is a personal concern, and in the practice of silence they find the satisfaction their hearts crave.   In like manner, the Salvation Army, which has pioneered in the gracious task of evangelism, has never observed the sacraments.   The Army, of course, does not claim to be a Church, but in its ranks are stalwart and heroic Christians whose spiritual life is fed at the deep springs of personal communion with God.   There are likewise many spiritually minded Christians to whom the sacraments make no appeal, who claim that all of life is sacramental and quote with approval Lowell's familiar lines:

> " The Holy Supper is kept, indeed,
> In whatso we share with another's need;
> Not what we give, but what we share,
> For the gift without the giver is bare;
> Who gives himself with his alms feeds three, —
> Himself, his hungering neighbor, and Me." [2]

Our authority must be the New Testament.   What is the teaching of the New Testament and what was the practice of the Apostolic Church?   When we open the records of the Early Church we are immediately confronted with the observance of the Christian sacraments.   There is no discussion, no debate, no controversy, but the immediate and unanimous acceptance of the practice of baptism and the observance of the Lord's Supper.   We have turned only a page or two in the history of the Church when we come face to face with the baptism of believers and the household celebration of the Lord's Supper.   Before the Gospels were written, before the Epistles were penned, before the conversion of Paul or the gathering in of the Gentiles, the early Christians were celebrating the sacraments, and the testimony of history is to the fact that there has never been a week, perhaps not a day, since Pentecost that the sacraments have not witnessed to the Christian faith.

This fact is worth emphasizing, for it bears in its keeping needed encouragement.   Together with the preaching of the

Word, the celebration of the sacraments has carried the Gospel message to the whole world. Preaching may sometimes fail. It often has failed. There are scholars who tell us that much of the preaching of our day bears little or no resemblance to the preaching of the Early Church. Professor C. H. Dodd goes so far as to say that " much of our preaching in Church at the present day would not have been recognized by the early Christians as *kerygma*." [3] Sounding the same challenge, Professor Hunter, of Mansfield College, says: " Preaching which finds the heart of the Gospel in, say, the Fatherhood of God, or the ethical principles of the Sermon on the Mount, must be regarded not as unchristian, but as a failure to ' continue stedfastly in the apostles' doctrine ' (Acts ii. 42). It is *didache;* but it is not *kerygma*. Not primarily in these terms did the apostles preach. Any preaching to-day which aims to be in line with the original Gospel must conserve the essential affirmations of the Apostolic preaching. Its core and kernel will be a story — a story that sounds as crazy to many of our wise men to-day as it did to the Greeks of Paul's day — a story centring in a Jew called Jesus the Messiah in whom the prophecies made of old to Israel were fulfilled, in whose life, death, resurrection, and exaltation the Living God acted conclusively for us men and our salvation." [4] There is, however, less occasion for failure in the celebration of the sacraments. They move within restricted limits. They are objective and and do not depend upon the preacher's " feelings " or upon his intellectual apprehensions. They proclaim the Gospel. They preach the *kerygma*. Baptism lays upon the celebrant the necessity of confessing the faith of the Triune God when he says, " I baptize thee in the name of the Father, and of the Son, and of the Holy Ghost." The sacrament of the Lord's Supper holds in its keeping, in its words, in its symbolism, in its administration, the very substance of the Christian faith. It does not reflect the thought of the age, or of any age, but speaks of " the Lamb of God, that taketh away the sin of the world." We listen to the strong words of Emil Brunner: " The Sacraments are the divinely given flying buttresses which save the Church from collapse. In how many of the churches of today do we not find the Sacraments almost the sole biblical footing — the only biblical element that has been able to withstand the caprices of the gifted minister who lives by his own wisdom rather than from the Scriptures. Even the most audacious minister has not dared to lay hands on the Sacraments. And they are what they are! One may so interpret the words of Scripture that the words speak the opposite of their intent; but the Sacraments, thank God, speak a language independent of the language of the pastor. They are a part of the message of the Church least affected by theological or other tendencies; and that is their especial blessing." [5]

Before the apostles began their missionary work, before the New Testament was written, before there was any bishop in Rome or Constantinople, the sacraments were proclaiming the Gospel; and ever since, in cathedral and chapel, in the open and in the catacombs, in prisons and concentration camps, they have been vocal with the Gospel message. The note of *penitence* is here, a penitence that deepens with more intimate knowledge of the life and death of our Lord. The note of *forgiveness* is here. In what has been called " the most intensely Christian of all liturgical texts " our need finds expression in the prayer:

" O Lamb of God, that takest away the sins of the world, have mercy
    upon us.
  O Lamb of God, that takest away the sins of the world, have mercy
    upon us.
  O Lamb of God, that takest away the sins of the world, grant us
    Thy peace."

The note of *thanksgiving* is here. The sacrament of the Lord's Supper is the Eucharist, the thanksgiving, for while we proclaim the sacrifice and death of our Lord, we celebrate also his risen life and his coming again. The note of *faith* is here. In the sacraments Christians, as with one voice, make confession of their faith either in the language of the Apostles' Creed,

" I believe in God the Father Almighty," or in the words of
the Nicene Creed, which is common to both Eastern and
Western Churches, " I believe in One God, the Father Almighty."

It is for this reason that Calvin concludes that there are two
sacraments and only two. They alone do what the Word of
God does. They proclaim the Gospel. " There can," he says,
" be no sacrament unaccompanied with a promise of salvation. All mankind, collected in one assembly, can promise us
nothing respecting our salvation. Therefore they can never
institute or establish a sacrament." [6] The word itself, however, was not so restricted in the history of the Church. Tertullian (160–230) speaks of the sacraments of " water, oil and
bread " and of " the sacrament of monogamy." Sometimes
he speaks of " the sacraments of faith," of " the resurrection,"
of " unction." Augustine calls the salt, administered before
baptism, a sacrament. Bernard called the rite of washing feet
a sacrament. In the twelfth century Hugo of St. Victor published his work, *On the Sacraments,* in which he announced
that there were six sacraments of varying degrees of importance, baptism and the Eucharist being of supreme value, because necessary to salvation. Later he declared that since there
are seven sins there must be seven sacraments, although he
names only six: baptism, confirmation, the Eucharist, penance,
last unction, and matrimony. Peter Lombard (1150) named
the seventh " ordination." To this number the Roman Church
and likewise the Eastern Church in their creeds and councils
have adhered.

In seeking to establish its position in giving sacramental
authority to these seven sacred acts the Roman Church has
sought assiduously to present reasons for the claim. There
must be seven sacraments because of the " analogy that exists
between natural and spiritual life. In order to exist, to preserve existence, and to contribute to his own and to the public
good, seven things seem necessary to man — to be born — to
grow — to be nurtured — to be cured when sick — when

weak to be strengthened — as far as regards the public weal, to have magistrates invested with authority to govern — and, finally to perpetuate himself and his species by legitimate off-spring." [7]

What, then, are these " seven things necessary to man "? It will be best to let the Roman Church speak for itself. " First of all, there is *Baptism,* the gate, as it were, to all the other sacraments, by which we are born again to Christ. The next is *Confirmation,* by which we grow up, and are strengthened in the grace of God: for, as St. Augustine observes, ' to the Apostles who have already received baptism, the Redeemer said: " stay you in the city till you be indued with power from on high." ' The third is the *Eucharist,* that true bread from heaven which nourishes our souls to eternal life, according to these words of the Saviour: ' My flesh is meat indeed, and my blood is drink indeed.' The fourth is *Penance,* by which the soul, which has caught the contagion of sin, is restored to spiritual health. The fifth is *Extreme Unction,* which obliterates the traces of sin, and invigorates the powers of the soul; of which St. James says: ' If he be in sins, they shall be forgiven him.' The sixth is *Holy Orders,* which gives power to perpetuate in the Church the public administration of the Sacraments, and the exercise of all the sacred functions of the ministry. The seventh and last is *Matrimony,* a sacrament instituted for the legitimate and holy union of man and woman for the human race, and the education of children, in the knowledge of religion, and the love and fear of God." [8] While holding to seven sacraments the Roman Church makes distinctions and assigns some to a lower and some to a higher order. " All and each of the Sacraments, it is true, possess an admirable efficacy given them by God: but it is well worthy of remark, that all are not of equal necessity or of equal dignity, nor is the signification of all the same. Amongst them three are of paramount necessity, a necessity, however, which arises from different causes. The universal and absolute necessity of baptism, these words of the Redeemer unequivocally declare: —

'Unless a man be born again of water and the Holy Ghost, he cannot enter into the kingdom of God.' The necessity of penance is relative: Penance is necessary for those only who have stained their baptismal innocence by mortal guilt: without sincere repentance, their eternal ruin is inevitable. Orders, too, although not necessary to each of the faithful, are of absolute general necessity to the Church. But, the dignity of the Sacraments considered, the Eucharist, for holiness, and for the number and greatness of its mysteries, is eminently superior to all the rest." [9]   In thus stating the primacy of the Lord's Supper the Church of Rome expresses, also, the position of evangelical Christianity.

It has been the teaching of Protestantism that the sacraments have the same function as the Word of God. Together they proclaim the Gospel and present Christ to us. For this reason, when either the Word or the sacraments are obscured there is necessarily an obscuring of the Gospel message. Something is lost. When, therefore, we find that one of the most popular and widely circulated books on Christian theology never makes mention of the sacraments, there is cause for concern.[10]   One is caught between such an absence of interest in things essential and an undue emphasis that causes some of our brethren to be called sacramentarians, so highly do they exalt the sacraments. We are reminded of Bishop Gore's humorous remark that there are people who believe in the blessed sacrament who do not seem to believe in Almighty God. We shall be saved from both extremes if we remember that " the office of the sacraments is precisely the same as that of the word of God; which is to offer and present Christ to us, and in him the treasures of his heavenly grace. . . . The sacraments . . . fulfil to us, on the part of God, the same office as messengers of joyful intelligence, or earnests for the confirmation of covenants on the part of men." [11]

In completeness and simplicity the sacraments present to us the Gospel of our salvation. Baptism is the rite of entrance

into the Christian Church. It is the believer's first act of
faith. It signs and seals him as one of the followers of Christ,
and opens the door into the company of the faithful. He becomes a member of the Christian community, the brotherhood
of believers. It marks him a child of the Kingdom. It sets
his feet in the way of salvation. On the other hand, the Lord's
Supper is his continuing nourishment along the way of his pil-
grimage. Thus baptism is once administered, but the Lord's
Supper is to be celebrated to the end of time. Baptism is the
initiation into the society of the faithful, and marks the definite commitment of life to Christ. Martin Luther was frequently tried and tempted in his faith, and in his darker hours
he would turn upon himself and his Tempter repeating the
words, " *Baptizatus sum, baptizatus sum*," " I have been baptized." The remembrance of that decisive act when his life
was committed to God in the sacrament of baptism brought
renewal of faith and courage. It gave him confidence and
support in the hour of weakness, for as the Confession of Faith
affirms " the efficacy of Baptism is not tied to that moment
of time wherein it is administered." [12] It has abiding value,
and this value consists largely in the recognition that at such
and such a time a decision was made, a commitment was regis-
tered which was accepted and sealed by the Holy Spirit.

The Christian life, however, is more than a beginning, more
than a decision once made, more than an action taken. The
Christian life is a life, and life needs constant nourishment.
It was of this that Paul was thinking when he used the illustration of the water that flowed in sustaining and refreshing
efficacy from the smitten rock: " They drank of a spiritual
rock that followed them: and the rock was Christ." [13] It was
of this that our Lord was thinking when he said, " I am the
living bread." [14] It is of this that the great sacramental hymns
of the Church are constantly reminding us. The words that
come to us out of the eleventh century give expression to the
constant need of the soul:

" We taste Thee, O Thou living Bread,
And long to feast upon Thee still;
We drink of Thee, the Fountainhead,
And thirst our souls from Thee to fill."

It was of this that John Bunyan was thinking when he told
the inimitable story of the Palace Beautiful which was set in
the way of Christian, the Pilgrim.   Bunyan was of course
speaking of the Church and the Sacrament of the Lord's Supper, but the reality is obscured by the luxuriance of the symbolism.   From the Palace Beautiful the Pilgrim could see Im-
manuel's Land " beautiful with woods, fruits of every sort,
flowers also, with springs and fountains."   There in that place
of peace and Christian fellowship the Supper was spread, and
there all the talk was of " the Lord of the hill; . . . what
he had done, and wherefore he did what he did."   It was conversation that centered upon the sacrifice of Christ, rather
upon Christ himself, and there the conversation continued
until late at night when the Pilgrim was laid to rest " in a large
upper chamber, whose windows opened towards the sunrising.
The name of the chamber was Peace."

From this point of view, we understand how the worship
of the Early Church took form under the inspiration of the
sacraments.   Baptism became the initiatory rite to the Christian Church.   It became the sign and seal of the new life in
Christ.   It initiated the baptized person into a new society —
the Christian Church.   It presupposed the acceptance of faith
in the Triune God, which form of expression was later expanded into the Catholic creeds.   On the other hand, the
Lord's Supper became the norm of Christian worship.   Side by
side with worship in the synagogue and in the Temple, which
was long continued by the early Christians, there developed
what has been called household worship.   We read that " day
by day, continuing stedfastly with one accord in the temple,
and breaking bread at home, they took their food with gladness and singleness of heart." [15]   They saw no inconsistency
in worshiping in the Temple, and in breaking bread at home.

" They continued stedfastly in the apostles' teaching and fellowship, in the breaking of bread and the prayers." [16] Gradually the Temple worship became less frequent as opposition and persecution developed, and the Lord's Supper observed in the homes of believers became the central service of Christian worship.

It would be easy to reconstruct those primitive services as held in Christian homes, for we have not only information contained in the New Testament but also the more definite outlines given in the postapostolic writers, such as the author of the *Didache* and Justin Martyr. We think of a large room, simply furnished, the women sitting apart from the men. The first meetings were doubtless held in secret and perhaps something like a password was necessary for admission, or one friend would introduce another. The service was led by the president, who had been selected, perhaps a presbyter or elder. He would begin with the reading of a passage from the Old Testament, from the Prophets, and, later, readings from what is now the New Testament would be heard. Then he would give what we call an exposition or interpretation of the passage and at the same time would present the facts of the Christian faith. Then followed the common prayers offered by the people themselves, and afterward they saluted " one another with a holy kiss." [17] The celebration of the Lord's Supper in its simplest form followed. Bread and wine mixed with water were brought in by the presbyters, or elders, and placed upon the table in front of the president, moderator, or bishop, who, taking them in his hands, began the sacramental prayer. In the *Didache* we have this prayer which is a very old thanksgiving: " We thank Thee, our Father, for the holy vine of David Thy servant which Thou hast made known to us through Jesus Thy servant; to Thee be the glory forever. And concerning the broken bread: We thank Thee, our Father, for the life and the knowledge which Thou hast made known to us through Jesus Thy servant; to Thee be the glory forever. Just as this broken bread was scattered over the hills and having been gathered together became one, so let Thy church be gathered together from the ends of the earth into Thy kingdom; for thine is the glory and the power through Jesus Christ forever." [18]   The prayer was usually cast in the form of a chant, a hymn of praise and thanksgiving.   According to Justin Martyr, the president or moderator " offers up praise and glory to the Father of the universe through the name of the Son and the Holy Spirit, and gives thanks at length that we have been accounted worthy of these things from Him; and when he has ended the prayers and thanksgiving the whole people present assent, saying ' Amen.' " [19]   He then took the elements and gave the broken bread and the cup to the presbyters, who distributed them to the congregation present.   When the distribution was finished, baskets were brought in and the elements were placed therein and taken by the presbyters to those who had not been able to be in attendance, and thus the service was completed.

In its simplest form this was the nature of the household worship in the Early Church.   Doubtless many other features were added.   Paul, in his discourse concerning speaking with tongues (I Cor., ch. 14), opens many windows for us to look in upon the worshiping congregation.   It is not all orderly.   There is some confusion.   There was, however, unity in regard to the central service of the Eucharist.   It was central in every service and around it gathered the worshipers of the Early Church.   " This food," says Justin Martyr, " is called among us the Eucharist, of which no one is allowed to partake but he who believes that the things which we teach are true, and who has been washed with the washing that is for the remission of sins and unto regeneration, and who is so living as Christ hath enjoined.   For we do not receive these elements as common bread and common drink, but in like manner as Jesus Christ our Saviour, having been made flesh by the word of God, had both flesh and blood for our salvation, so likewise have we been taught that the food which is blessed by the prayer of the word which comes from Him, and from which our blood and flesh are nourished by transmutation, is the flesh and blood of that Jesus who was made flesh." [20]

We are concerned here, not with the interpretation of the Eucharist, but with the fact that in the Early Church Christian worship was organized around the Eucharist. The Reformers did not set this standard aside, and Calvin wished to preserve the observance of the Lord's Supper every Sunday. Dr. Maxwell in his exhaustive study of the form of worship carried on in Geneva says: " Our Service [i.e., the worship service of the Church of Scotland] is based historically upon the central Service of Christendom, and care should be taken to preserve that great tradition. All reform of our present services should be based upon the Eucharist, and not upon Morning Prayer in the *Book of Common Prayer*. Morning Prayer is a daily service, and has no relation to our rites. The Sunday Service should be based upon what is central, Catholic, and evangelical, and in scope and content should follow the Eucharist." [21]

The word " liturgy " in its ecclesiastical sense refers to the service of Holy Communion. It may not be possible for all Churches to return to the weekly observance of the Sacrament, but it is possible to see to it that worship " in scope and content " follows the movements connected with the celebration of the Lord's Supper. That is to say, worship should always possess the qualities we recognize as belonging to the Eucharist service. There will be recognition in an act of adoration of what God has done. There will be the response of glad thanksgiving for all that God has done and still is doing. There will be the recognition that we are not alone, but are doing something together as a community of believers. There will be the proclamation of the Gospel as in the words of institution. There will be the offering up of ourselves, a living sacrifice. There will be the exercise of a living, appropriating, justifying faith that lays hold of the things of God. In all the worship, in Scripture, song, prayer, and sermon, there will be the constant and unfailing recognition that the Gospel is a " given thing." We will hear a voice saying: " A new heart will I give unto you. . . . This is my body. . . . Take, eat." Always and in every part of the service we will take from his hand. Always and in every part of the service we will be saying, " Thanks be to God for his unspeakable gift."

III. Baptism in the New Testament

WHEN we open the New Testament we are face to face with the practice of baptism. The story of the life of our Lord begins with the baptism of John, the forerunner. After the brief account of the birth of Jesus, Matthew tells us that John was carrying on his ministry and that the people " were baptized of him in the river Jordan, confessing their sins." [1] We are told that Jesus himself came to be baptized of John. No surprise is expressed concerning the rite as practiced by John. Apparently it was accepted and its meaning clearly understood. It was symbolic of purification. Mark's Gospel plunges into the public ministry of Jesus and almost without introduction states that " John came, who baptized in the wilderness and preached the baptism of repentance unto remission of sins." [2] Baptism was recognized by the people as related to moral cleansing, the beginning of a new life under God's guiding hand. The Gospel of Luke enlarges on John's methods and mission, but in insisting upon baptism there is no suggestion that the people held back because it was something novel or outside the customs of their own religion. John " came into all the region round about the Jordan, preaching the baptism of repentance unto remission of sins." [3] Each Gospel repeats the practice of the rite and gives it the same interpretation. It was a symbol of cleansing. The Fourth Gospel is very explicit and the influence of John's ministry is emphasized: " For this cause came I baptizing in water." [4]

When the New Testament opens, before Jesus began his ministry, before the Gospel was preached, baptism by water was being administered. No surprise was expressed and no questions asked. The people were accustomed to see the rite administered. When a Jewish delegation came to John saying, " Why then baptizest thou, if thou art not the Christ, neither Elijah, neither the prophet? " [5] they did not question the meaning or purpose of the rite, but they did question the authority by which John practiced it. Later in the ministry of our Lord, when Jesus was asked the source of his authority, he replied by asking his critics a question which they themselves had previously raised: " The baptism of John, whence was it? from heaven or from men? " [6] They were unwilling to answer, but no question was raised concerning the practice of the rite itself or its moral significance. Before Christianity became a religion, baptism was recognized and practiced.

Baptism as a symbol of cleansing has been widely used. We find it in the ethnic faiths. It was practiced in Greece and Rome, among Hindus and Mohammedans, Sikhs and Parsis. It was the initiatory rite into the so-called mystery religions, and there have been scholars who have traced the Christian sacramental rites to this source. The old religions of Greece and Rome were decadent and the mystery cults were eagerly welcomed, not only by those who had been accustomed to worship at the altars of paganism, but especially by those who hungered and thirsted for some deeper experience of the spiritual life. These new religions, with their symbolism, their appeal to the mystical and mysterious, their demand for absolute surrender, had made great headway among the people and had adopted language and rites singularly akin to those used in the Christian Church. They practiced a secret and exclusive initiation followed by fellowship limited to the initiated. They were a separated, exclusive group. Their worship was closed to all outsiders. No one could enter, even as an observer, who had not been ceremoniously welcomed. Their secrets were well kept, and even today we do not know surely what went on behind those closed doors. Nevertheless, we know something, for recent literature has given us vivid descriptions of what is supposed to have taken place in the secret circles of the mystery cults.

The rite of initiation was practiced under a form of baptism or purification or ceremonial cleansing. Without moral cleanliness no one could approach the holy place. From Origen we get the formula which was in use: " Let no one enter whose hands are not clean and whose tongue is not prudent." It is said that Nero sought membership in the mystery cult of Eleusis, but was deterred by the stringency of the moral demands, for those demands called for repentance and full confession of sin. After such self-purification the candidate was bathed in pure water and thus became a new creature. This rite of initiation by baptism was followed by a second sacrament which admitted to full membership. The ceremony consisted of fasting and afterward the partaking of a sacred sacrificial meal, which was observed with impressive ritual and elaborate symbolism.

It is natural, because of the intimate parallelism existing between the rites of these mystery cults and the sacraments of the Christian Church, that many scholars should be led to accept the view that they were mutually dependent, and indeed the view has been widely held by competent writers that the Christian sacraments were an outgrowth of the mystery cults. Scholarship today, however, is less inclined to accept such a position. The evidence we have is meager, and it is easy enough to build an impressive argument on scanty premises. The opinion is gaining ground that, instead of the mystery religions' influencing the teaching and language of the New Testament, it is more likely that the prestige of the Christian faith influenced the ritual of the pagan mysteries. Justin Martyr, for example, charged that Mithraism, which had a closer kinship to the Christian sacraments than other cults, developed too late to have influenced Christianity and therefore must have used Christian customs to its own advantage. Indeed Bishop Brilioth comes to the definite conclusion that " the attempt to derive baptism and the eucharist directly from heathen rites is now seen to be one of the freaks of historical scholarship and a symptom of a childish ailment, which is not uncommon in young sciences. Today this theory appears only in the popular expositions, whose mission seems to be to grant a further lease of life to the less fortunate hypotheses of real scholars. Serious discussion is now confined to the date and the extent of the influence of the mystery religions on the Christian sacrament." [7]

We are on surer ground when we relate the baptism of John to the rites and symbolism of the Old Testament and to the practice of proselyte baptism of John's own time. The idea of symbolic purification pervades the entire ritual of Judaism. All who had been defiled were commanded to immerse before they offered sacrifice. Indeed, not only persons but things are spoken of as being subject to " baptismal " cleansing. In the ancient ritual of the tabernacle the Lord commanded Moses saying: " Thou shalt also make a laver of brass, and the base thereof of brass, whereat to wash. And thou shalt put it between the tent of meeting and the altar, and thou shalt put water therein. And Aaron and his sons shall wash their hands and their feet thereat: when they go into the tent of meeting, they shall wash with water." [8] The rite of cleansing became a part of the religious ceremony of the Hebrew people, and when in time, like other ceremonies, it became formal and meaningless the prophets began to speak of an inner cleansing, a purification of the heart, and sounded forth a call to repentance and personal dedication. " I will sprinkle clean water upon you, and ye shall be clean: from all your filthiness, and from all your idols, will I cleanse you. A new heart also will I give you, and a new spirit will I put within you; and I will take away the stony heart out of your flesh, and I will give you a heart of flesh." [9]

Furthermore, between the Old and the New Testaments there had grown up what is called " proselyte baptism." With the decay of the pagan religions and the craving for spiritual reality that was unsatisfied, many of the thoughtful people of both Greece and Rome found satisfaction in the monotheism of Israel, with its emphasis on the inner life, its moral ideal, and its holy God. It is not surprising that many Gentiles sought fellowship in the religion of Israel. They were called

" proselytes," which is the Greek word for the Hebrew " resident aliens." They were received into the fellowship of Israel through a ceremony of initiation, in which baptism had a prominent place. The reception of proselytes took place in the presence of witnesses, and they were admitted by the threefold rites of circumcision, baptism, and sacrifice. After circumcision the man was taken to the bath, and while he stood in the water the rabbis recited in his hearing some of the commandments of the Jewish law, and then, after being completely immersed in water, he came forth a new creature into the fellowship of the faithful. The ceremony thus became, not only a symbol of purification from heathenism, but the mode of admission into the ranks of the people of God. The proselyte became through baptism a member of a new society, a citizen with his Jewish brethren in the commonwealth of Israel, the people of God. Rabbi Joseph Klausner, in his latest book *From Jesus to Paul*, says: " Ablution was an ancient custom in Israel. All ancient peoples were wont to practise ablution for bodily and spiritual cleanness. Jewish ablution was based, no doubt, on these verses: ' And I will sprinkle clean water upon you, and ye shall be clean; from all your uncleannesses, and from all your idols, will I cleanse you. A new heart also will I give you, and a new spirit will I put within you; and I will take away the stony heart out of your flesh, and I will give you a heart of flesh.' Thus was ablution for both male and female proselytes customary in Israel. By means of the ablution they were, so to speak, cleansed from all their pagan ' uncleannesses,' while receiving ' a new heart ' and ' a new spirit.' Indeed, the male proselyte, who was circumcised and baptized, and the female proselyte, who was only baptized, became ' as newborn children.' " [10]

It was natural then that John, in the fulfillment of his divine mission, should lay hold of baptism as the rite of initiation into the new social order of righteousness. Jesus continued the practice but gave to it a new significance. John himself recognized the difference when he said, " I indeed baptize you in water unto repentance: but he that cometh after me is mightier than I, whose shoes I am not worthy to bear: he shall baptize you in the Holy Spirit and in fire." [11]   Many New Testament scholars, among them Professor T. W. Manson, believe that this statement by John had at the first no reference to the Holy Spirit.   The doctrine of the Holy Spirit was a later development.   The Early Church, however, after Pentecost did identify baptism by " fire " with the Holy Spirit, and that identification appears now in the New Testament text. The words used by John fitted into his own ministry of judgment.   " He shall baptize you . . . in fire " means that the wrath of God would fall upon an unrepentant nation.   Professor Manson says: " So long as the Holy Spirit is retained, John's words are a promise: my baptism is a prelude to a better.   When the reference to the Spirit is dropped, the true nature of the saying is apparent.   It falls into line with the rest of John's preaching.   The baptism with fire is parallel to the other references to fire and to be understood in the same way. The sense of the saying is, not that John's baptism is the preliminary to something better, but that it is the last chance of escaping something very much worse, namely the coming judgement."   Continuing, he says: " In this setting the baptism of John can perhaps be most readily understood by reference to the Jewish baptism of proselytes.   As the baptism of the proselyte was part of the ceremony of dedication by which a Gentile was incorporated into Israel, so John's baptism is an act of rededication by which Israelites, who through sin have lost their right to the name, may be incorporated afresh into the true Israel." [12]

The baptism of John was symbolic.   It symbolized the washing away of the past, and the rebirth of Israel's covenant relationship.   The baptism of Jesus was sacramental, symbolizing the washing away of the past and through the Holy Spirit sealing to believers the benefits, not of the covenant of Israel, but of the new covenant of grace.   That this difference was clear to the Church of the New Testament is revealed in the record given concerning Paul's encounter with certain disciples of John at Ephesus. There he met twelve men who had received baptism. They may have been baptized by John himself or by some of John's disciples, although Luke speaks of them as " certain disciples " and Paul, recognizing their faith, asked the question: " Did ye receive the Holy Spirit when ye believed? And they said unto him, Nay, we did not so much as hear whether the Holy Spirit was given. And he said, Into what then were ye baptized? And they said, Into John's baptism. And Paul said, John baptized with the baptism of repentance, saying unto the people that they should believe on him that should come after him, that is, on Jesus. And when they heard this, they were baptized into the name of the Lord Jesus." [13]

Just as Jesus took the Jewish Passover and transformed it into the Lord's Supper, giving it a new interpretation, so he took the rite of baptism, long practiced in Israel, and gave it a new significance. In his hands it became a sacrament, the sign and seal of new life in him. It is worthy of note in the case of both the sacraments that they were instituted by Christ only when his redemptive work was nearing completion, and this fact may account for the statement in the Fourth Gospel that " Jesus himself baptized not, but his disciples." [14] The disciples continued the symbolic baptism inaugurated by John, but Christian baptism presupposes the finished work of Christ. Indeed the references to baptism in the Gospels are meager and sometimes uncertain. Great stress has often been put on our Lord's words to Nicodemus: " Except one be born of water and the Spirit, he cannot enter into the kingdom of God." [15] The words are, in a sense, enigmatic, and it is only as we look back that they take on sacramental significance. The words, says Bishop Westcott, " look forward to the fulness of the Christian dispensation, when after the Resurrection the baptism of water was no longer separated from, but united with, the baptism of the spirit in the ' laver of regeneration ' (Titus iii.5. Comp. Eph. v.26), even as the outward and the inward are united generally in a religion which is sacramental and not only typical." [16]

The words to which the institution of baptism is usually tied occur in the great passage at the close of the Gospel narrative and belong to the post-Resurrection narratives. According to Matthew, Jesus said, " All authority hath been given unto me in heaven and on earth. Go ye therefore, and make disciples of all the nations, baptizing them into the name of the Father and of the Son and of the Holy Spirit." [17] In the disputed ending of Mark's Gospel we read: " Go ye into all the world, and preach the gospel to the whole creation. He that believeth and is baptized shall be saved; but he that disbelieveth shall be condemned." [18] The reference in Matthew has occasioned questioning, not on account of any doubtful manuscript authority, but because of the use of the Trinitarian formula, which seems to imply a later theological development. It is impossible to enter upon a critical analysis here. The conclusion reached by Professor Manson represents the best scholarship of our day: " The Trinitarian baptismal formula, possibly introduced into the text of this Gospel because it was used in baptizing in the Church where this Gospel circulated, could hardly have been uttered by Jesus Himself, since the Christian Church for many years after the death of Jesus never used that baptismal formula at all, but was satisfied to baptize converts into the name of the Lord Jesus alone." [19] Professor A. B. Bruce, in *The Expositor's Greek Testament*, says that " this great final word of Jesus is worthy of the Speaker and of the situation. Perhaps it is not to be taken as an exact report of what Jesus said to His disciples at a certain time and place. In it the real and the ideal seem to be blended; what Jesus said there and then with what the Church of the apostolic age had gradually come to regard as the will of their Risen Lord, with growing clearness as the years advanced, with perfect clearness after Israel's crisis had come." [20]

It did not take the Early Church long to accept the Trinitarian formula, for it occurs not only in Matthew but in the

Didache, which is dated in the early part of the second century: " Concerning baptism, thus baptize ye: having spoken beforehand of these things, baptize into the name of the Father and of the Son and of the Holy Ghost in living water." [21] It would seem, therefore, that even if the formula does not belong to the words of Jesus, it at least expresses his mind and the mind of the Primitive Church.

While the Trinitarian formula is not used elsewhere in the New Testament, it is implied in the more simple formula used in the Early Church. The apostles baptized in or into " the name of the Lord Jesus." As the Christology of the Church developed, the Trinitarian formula would express for first-century Christians what was meant by baptism " in the name of Jesus." That this was the earliest formula may be discovered by even a superficial reading of The Acts and of the Epistles. On the Day of Pentecost Peter enjoined the people to " be baptized every one of you in the name of Jesus Christ." [22] When Peter and John went down to Samaria they discovered that disciples had been " baptized into the name of the Lord Jesus." [23] When Paul met with the twelve disciples at Ephesus, who knew only John's baptism, " they were baptized into the name of the Lord Jesus." [24] In the Epistle to the Romans, Paul asks the question, " Are ye ignorant that all we who were baptized into Christ Jesus were baptized into his death? " [25] To the Galatians he wrote, " As many of you as were baptized into Christ did put on Christ." [26] We can see the movement toward the expansion of this early baptismal formula in Paul's letter to the Church at Corinth, in a passage where there is an undoubted reference to baptism: " But ye were washed, but ye were sanctified, but ye were justified in the name of the Lord Jesus Christ, and in the Spirit of our God." [27] Certainly the words, " In the name of the Lord Jesus Christ, and in the Spirit of our God," appearing in this First Epistle to the Corinthians, are a near approach to the Trinitarian formula found in Matthew. Between them there is a close resemblance both in language and in meaning.

To be baptized in or into " the name of the Lord Jesus " is to be spiritually identified with Christ himself. It was for this reason Paul indignantly set aside all tendency to schism in the Christian Church. To the Corinthians who were disposed to sectional tendencies he said, " Were ye baptized into the name of Paul? " [28] Certainly not. They were baptized, not into the name of Paul, or Apollos, or Cephas, but into the name of Christ. This consecrating act made them one with Christ. It identified them with Christ. It became the bond which bound all Christians in the fellowship of " One Lord, one faith, one baptism, one God and Father of all, who is over all, and through all, and in all." [29]

To be baptized " into Christ " or " in the name of the Lord Jesus " is to be identified with Christ, and it is in this sense that baptism is used in the New Testament. It is this that differentiates Christian baptism from John's baptism and from all other baptism. Thus there is something more implied in Christian baptism than symbolic cleansing and the New Testament turns to varying forms of expression to make this fact clear: " As many of you as were baptized into Christ did put on Christ." [30] " Having been buried with him in baptism, wherein ye were also raised with him through faith." [31] " All we who were baptized into Christ Jesus were baptized into his death." [32] The language suggests rebirth. The old has passed and, behold, all things have become new. " Salvation from sin, from pessimism, from the sense that all things pass in inevitable destruction, from materialism, is not for us Christians to be attained by dreaming of a world beyond this world, or by believing in some imminent catastrophe, but by plunging head first into Christian faith and fellowship." [33] And to plunge " head first into Christian faith and fellowship " is what is signified by Christian baptism. The ritual of the Eastern Orthodox Church furnishes striking evidence of the significance of this act of identification with Christ in baptism. The priest speaking to the person to be baptized says thrice, " Dost thou unite thyself unto Christ? " and thrice he answers, " I do."

Again the priest says, " Hast thou united thyself unto Christ? " Thrice the question is asked and thrice the answer is given, " I have." Later in the service the priest again asks, " Hast thou united thyself unto Christ? " and again thrice the response is made, " I have," and the priest answers, " Bow down also before Him." [34] It is an act of identification, of union with Christ through the sacrament.

If we could recover something of the radiancy of early Christianity, baptism might become to us the sign and seal of the joy of the Lord and the peace of his salvation. According to Tertullian the celebration of the sacrament of baptism took place at one of the great festivals of the Church, usually on Easter Day. The catechumens had given in their names, had been instructed in the Christian faith, had memorized the creed given them. They had been taught the Lord's Prayer and then, having put on white garments and wearing baptismal wreaths and chaplets, they were baptized " in the name of the Father and of the Son and of the Holy Ghost." It was a festive occasion. It was the entrance into a new life, a life in Christ and with Christ's people. There was a note of triumph in every step taken. Thus baptism ought to be for us, and for our children. Instead of being a " name-giving service," a christening, an external act of conformity, it should be the occasion of a glad and unforgettable experience. A true realization of the meaning and significance of Christian baptism as an act of God, and a responsive act of man, would bring to us the inexpressible joy that welled up in the heart of Augustine when he said: " Too late loved I Thee, O Thou Beauty of ancient days, yet ever new! Too late I loved Thee! " [35]

IV. The Sacrament of Christian Baptism

THE New Testament consistently sets forth baptism as the commitment of life to Christ. It is a public confession of faith and the rite of initiation into the Christian community. In the Old Testament economy circumcision was the sign of the covenant relation between God and his people. In the Christian Church baptism became the sign of the new covenant. It marked the dividing line between the non-Christian and the Christian. Baptism became the sign and seal of the new life in Christ and the new fellowship with the followers of Christ. Every extension of the boundaries of the Christian Church was marked by the administration of this rite. When the Gospel began its triumphant career on the Day of Pentecost, Peter bade the people, " Be baptized every one of you." When the Gospel entered Samaria, the Samaritans were " baptized . . . in the name of the Lord Jesus." Philip, after winning the Ethiopian to Christ, immediately received him into the Christian fellowship through baptism. Paul, converted to Christianity, " arose and was baptized." Cornelius, and after him the Gentile world, was admitted to the Christian Church after baptism, thus marking the new faith as embracing people of all the world. The faith of the Roman jailer at Philippi was followed by baptism of himself and his whole house. The letters of Paul to the Churches at Rome, Corinth, Ephesus, Galatia, Colossae testify to the unity of the Church that possessed " one Lord, one faith, one baptism."

Evangelical Christians have always asserted that the mark of a sacrament is that it was instituted by Christ himself. And that statement seems to be authenticated by the practice of the apostles, who, immediately after Pentecost, began to observe

both baptism and the Lord's Supper. Of course those who
maintain that there are other sacraments besides baptism and
the Lord's Supper can also find New Testament support for
their position. They quote Paul as saying that he and others
with him were " ministers of Christ, and stewards of the mysteries of God," the " mysteries of God " being the sacraments,
the number not being named. They maintain that extreme
unction must have been instituted by Christ and that in his
epistle James merely expounds it. In like manner, confirmation was inherent in the promise of the outpouring of the Holy
Spirit which was fulfilled on the Day of Pentecost. The sacraments of penance and confession follow from the giving of
the keys of the Kingdom to Peter as head of the Church. Such
New Testament references, however, are not sufficient to lift
these actions into sacramental significance. To infer that
Christ instituted Unction as a sacrament from the reference
to anointing the sick with oil, confirmation from the promised coming of the Holy Spirit, and penance and confession
from the bestowal of the " keys " to Peter, goes beyond the
meaning of the words of Scripture. Furthermore, the practice of the Apostolic Church points to the fact that only baptism and the Lord's Supper had sacramental value to the early
Christians.

Not only are there separating differences between the Protestant interpretation and that of the Roman and Greek Catholic Churches regarding the number of the sacraments, but there
is a critical difference as to the nature of the sacraments themselves. The evangelical position has always attributed the efficacy of the sacraments to the total sacramental act and to the
faith by which the sacrament is received. The Roman and
Greek interpretation gives efficacy to the consecrated elements
— water, bread, and wine. The Roman Church believes that
the sacraments are efficacious *ex opere operato*, that is to say, by
their own inherent value; while evangelicals hold that they
have virtue *ex opere operantis*, that is, through the faith of
him who partakes of them. The difference may be simpli-

fied by quoting from a prayer taken from the Ethiopic Stat-
utes of the Apostles: " God, my Lord almighty, who madest
heaven and earth . . . who mingledst and unitedst the immortal with the mortal, who madest living man a combination
of the two, and gavest to that which was made body a soul also,
which thou causest to dwell within: stir this water and fill it
up with thy Holy Spirit, that it may become water and Spirit
for regeneration to those who are to be baptized: work a holy
work and make them to become sons and daughters of thy
holy name." [1] Such petitions are common in early liturgies
and were inspired by the philosophy of that day, that a spirit,
good or bad, could enter and possess things material. Modern
thought and present-day experience, however, tend to dis-
countenance such supposed interpenetration of the divine. We
do not see the sacraments working *ex opere operato*. What we
do see is the evident fact that to those who receive the sacraments by faith there is manifest blessing.

The problem, however, is not easily elucidated and eventu-
ally we come into the realm of controversy. We have become
accustomed to the ritual service of the Eucharist, in which,
in a consecrating prayer the minister says: " We pray Thee to
bless and sanctify with Thy Word and Spirit these Thine own
gifts of Bread and Wine which we set before Thee, that we
may receive by faith Christ crucified for us, and so feed upon
Him that He may be made one with us and we with Him." [2]
We are accustomed to this ritual, and yet who can interpret
or exhaust the meaning of words such as, " Sanctify these elements both of Bread and Wine "? What is the difference between the elements that are not " sanctified " and those that
are? Is the difference in the things per se, or is it in the mind
of the worshiper, who sees beyond the things seen to the things
signified? Is the water also to be sanctified? The Roman
Church says " yes " and attributes to baptism the virtue of
regeneration. In the ritual of the Greek Orthodox Church
this prayer is offered: " Do thou, O Master, show the water to
be the water of redemption, the water of sanctification, the

purification of the flesh and spirit, the loosing of bonds, the remission of sins, the illumination of the soul, the laver of regeneration, the renewal of the Spirit of adoption to sonship, the garment of incorruption, the fountain of life." [3] One would think that on this subject, which is so important, indeed primary, Baptist Churches would have a satisfying literature interpreting their position. It is, however, difficult to put one's hand upon authoritative literature which presents the sacramental interpretation of baptism from the Baptist point of view. We are compelled to go to Strong's *Systematic Theology* and to its inadequate interpretation. Baptism is a symbol and nothing more. It expresses through the symbolism of water what has already taken place in the heart of the believer. Indeed the ritual of the sacrament of baptism used in the Presbyterian Church is almost wholly symbolic, and lacks the signature of the theology of that Church which affirms that baptism is not only a sign but a seal. The Presbyterian Order in the *Book of Common Worship*.

" Grant, O Lord, to these Thy servants grace to perform the things they have promised before Thee:

" And sanctify with Thy Spirit this Child now to be baptized according to Thy Word; through Jesus Christ our Lord. Amen." [4]

The ritual of the *Book of Common Order* of the Church of Scotland does not hesitate to use the same formula of consecration for the water as is used in the consecration of the bread and wine in the Communion Service. The Scottish ritual reads: " Sanctify this water to the spiritual use to which Thou hast ordained it; and grant that Thy servant, now to be baptized therewith, may receive the fullness of Thy grace, and ever remain in the number of Thy faithful people; through Jesus Christ our Lord. Amen." [5] This wording has the authority of the Westminster divines, who, in their Directory for Worship, say that after the exhortation by the minister " prayer is also to be joined with the word of institution, for sanctifying the water to this spiritual use; and the minister is to pray to this or the like effect: ' That the Lord, who hath not left us as strangers without the covenant of promise, but called us to the privileges of his ordinances, would graciously vouchsafe to sanctify and bless his own ordinance of baptism at this time: That he would join the inward baptism of his Spirit with the outward baptism of water; make this baptism to the infant a seal of adoption, remission of sin, regeneration, and eternal life, and all other promises of the covenant of grace: That the child may be planted into the likeness of the death and resurrection of Christ; and that, the body of sin being destroyed in him; he may serve God in newness of life all his days." [6]

When we come to interpret the words " sanctify this water," " join the inward baptism of His Spirit with the outward baptism of water," we stand on the threshold of what cannot be expressed in words. Perhaps it is for this reason that the Roman Church speaks of the sacraments as " mysteries." The English word, however, does not have a sacramental meaning, although it permits that Church to suggest to its people that in the sacrament there is a divine action which lies too deep for interpretation. There is truth in this position and we fall into intellectual difficulties when we seek to explain and precisely determine what the Holy Spirit does in the sacrament. The same situation faces us when we seek to reason out how the Holy Spirit makes effectual to salvation the reading of the Word. It would be a mistake, however, to give to the sacraments a mysterious role beyond the understanding or comprehension of those who administer and those who receive them. They are meant, not to obscure truth, but to elucidate and make manifest the will of God for our salvation. In them we see the Gospel even as we hear the Gospel through preaching.

When we are dealing with the work of God, anywhere in nature, in the human heart, in the Scriptures, or in the sacraments, we are always face to face with the mysterious. Who can tell how God paints one flower blue and another red? Who can tell how God begins the work of regeneration in the heart? Who can tell how God speaks through the Scriptures

to the awakening of one soul and the comfort of another?
Who can tell how the Holy Spirit moves through the sacrament, conveying grace to believers? " Verily thou art a God
that hidest thyself." And yet it is sure that God does work
in nature, in the heart, in the Word, and in the sacraments.
It belongs to the Christian experience to know what passeth
knowledge.

> " I know not how that Bethlehem's Babe
> Could in the Godhead be;
> I only know the Manger Child
> Has brought God's life to me." [7]

Probably the subject can be approached through the authorized formulas which express the mind of the Churches and
which make clear the controversies which have been so un-
fortunate. While the references used apply to the sacrament
of baptism, they may also interpret in a sense the attitude of
the respective Churches to the Eucharist. In the first place,
there are many Christians in all evangelical Churches who
look upon baptism, not as a sacrament, but as a symbol and
nothing more. The Swiss Reformer Zwingli held what may
be called a moral-influence theory similar to that which asserts
that the sacrament has representative and symbolic value only.
Zwingli was a puritan of a severe type. Thorough scholar and
faithful expositor of the Bible, he had no sympathy with any
form or ritual. Although like Luther and Calvin he was a
lover of music, he banished all music from the worship services of the Church, and the austere simplicity which he demanded still marks the services of the Swiss Church. He had
no tolerance of any view of the sacraments other than that
they were " bare signs." The sacraments he defined as akin to
a " national costume or badge " or other emblem that testified
that a man belonged to this or that nation or society. Although
the teaching of Zwingli has not been formulated into an accepted creed, as has that of Calvin and Luther, it cannot be
doubted that his point of view is held by multitudes in our
Christian Churches and has been sanctioned by many writers

and preachers. The Society of Friends disowns and discards all sacramental practices. The Salvation Army does not administer baptism or celebrate the Lord's Supper. The founder of the Army, William Booth, said, " We teach our soldiers that every time they break bread they are to remember the broken body of the Lord, and every time they wash the body they are to remind themselves of the cleansing power of the blood of Christ, of the indwelling of his Spirit." A professor in a Baptist theological college in interpreting the Baptist position claimed that the sacrament was " a pantomime," a visible symbol or sign representing a spiritual experience which already had taken place. When asked what God did in the baptismal act, he replied that God did nothing. The work of God had already been done, and baptism was merely the recognition of previous divine action.

John Calvin occupied a position between Zwingli and Luther, and the stamp of his teaching is upon the Reformed Churches, including the Anglican and Episcopal Communions. Calvin himself was not satisfied with the symbolic interpretation of baptism. In *The Institutes* he says: " The sacraments are attended with no benefit without the influence of the Holy Spirit; and that, in hearts already instructed by that Teacher, they still subserve the confirmation and increase of faith. There is only this difference that our eyes and ears are naturally endued with the faculties of seeing and hearing, but Christ accomplishes this in our hearts by special and preternatural grace." [8] He does not, however, specify what he means by " special and preternatural grace." He evidently meant that there was something in the sacraments not exhausted by thinking of them as mere signs. In interpreting the Reformed position, John Knox's *Book of Common Order*, in use in Scotland from 1564 to 1645, says: " Baptism was ordained to be ministered in the element of water, to teach us, that like as water outwardly doth wash away the filth of the body, so inwardly doth the virtue of Christ's blood purge our souls from that corruption and deadly poison, wherewith by nature we were infected, whose venomous dregs, although they continue in this our flesh, yet by the merits of his death are not imputed unto us, because the justice of Jesus Christ is made ours by Baptism, not that we think any such virtue or power to be included in the visible water, or outward action, for many have been baptised, and yet never inwardly purged; but that our Saviour Christ, who commanded Baptism to be ministered, will, by the power of His Holy Spirit, effectually work in the hearts of His Elect, in time convenient, all that is meant and signified by the same." [9] Knox, like Calvin, had nothing to do with assigning any virtue or power to the visible water but assures us that all that is " meant and signified " by the sacrament will be conveyed to true believers by the Holy Spirit. The Westminster Confession of Faith, seeking to make clear this same Calvinistic position, says: " The efficacy of Baptism is not tied to that moment of time wherein it is administered: yet, notwithstanding, by the right use of this ordinance the grace promised is not only offered, but really exhibited and conferred by the Holy Ghost." [10] Something is done. Something is given. Something is sealed to the believer. What is given belongs, says a Scottish theologian, to " the secret things of God. It is wiser to hold by that of which we can speak with great certainty. This much at least may be said of the grace of baptism, that therein the Holy Spirit is given, we may humbly believe, according to the capacity of the recipient at the moment, but assuredly as a pledged and covenanted gift ready to aid and guide us as soon as we are able to use His aid and guidance." [11]

Martin Luther, the dynamic leader of the Reformation, had no patience with the mere symbolic interpretation of baptism as presented by Zwingli and was not satisfied with Calvin's emphasis upon the Holy Spirit's working through the sacrament upon the hearts of believers. Luther believed that baptism did something, or rather that God did something, in baptism. Luther was never consistent, and his teaching on the sacraments at one time seems to suggest a " sign " value only and then again he seems to approach the Roman view of regeneration through baptism. His words, however, are not vague. We know what he is saying. "Baptism," he asserts, "is necessary for all, because Christ has commanded that all should be baptized, and has connected the blessing of salvation with this sacrament. Those who despise it and refuse to be baptized, cannot be saved. But if any person should desire baptism and be unable to obtain it, he would not on that account be lost. It is not the lack of baptism, but the despising of baptism that condemns." [12] Taken by itself this statement is highly sacramentarian, but Luther was too much committed to the doctrine of justification by faith to be accredited with teaching baptismal regeneration. "Baptism," he says, "is not simply water, but it is the water comprehended in God's command, and connected with God's Word. What is that Word of God? That which Christ, our Lord, says in the last chapter of Matthew — 'Go ye into all the world and teach all the nations, and baptize them into the name of the Father and of the Son and of the Holy Spirit.' What benefits does baptism confer? It works forgiveness of sins, delivers from death and the devil, and gives everlasting salvation to all who believe this, as the words and promises of God declare. Which are those words and promises of God? Those which Christ, our Lord, says in the last chapter of Mark — 'He that believeth and is baptized shall be saved; but he that believeth not shall be damned.' How can water do such great things? It is not water indeed that does it, but the Word of God, which is in and with the water, and faith which trusts this Word of God in the water. For without the Word of God the water is simply water, and no baptism. But with the Word of God, it is a baptism, that is a gracious water of life and a washing of regeneration in the Holy Spirit." [13] If, then, the question is asked, "What does God do in the sacrament?" Luther will say, "Everything," for "it is not man's baptism but Christ's and God's baptism which we receive from the hand of a man."

The Holy Orthodox Eastern Church, together with the Roman Church, holds that the sacrament "conveys to the soul of a faithful man, the invisible grace of God." When the administration of baptism takes place and the Christian formula is spoken, then salvation is sealed upon the heart of the recipient. Therefore baptism is necessary to all for salvation. The Roman Catholic Catechism states the position in clear language: "The Sacrament of Baptism is a Sacrament of cleansing instituted by Jesus Christ; by it the person baptized is made a member of the true church of Jesus Christ, obtains remission of original sin and of all actual sins if he has committed any, with all the punishment due to them, and becomes capable of receiving the other Sacraments." [14] To be baptized is to be regenerate, and because of this teaching, even in Augustine's day, baptism was often deferred till death was imminent, so that all sin would be washed away.

While there are differences in the various interpretations of the sacrament of baptism throughout the Christian Church, certain common characteristics belong to the ritual in all the Churches. Indeed, it may be said that Christian baptism is, in a very definite sense, a uniting bond throughout Christendom. In all evangelical and Catholic Churches it is the act of initiation into membership in the Christian fellowship. It is the sign and seal of the new covenant of grace which unites in a mystical bond the people of God throughout the whole world. It marks the break with the old life, and the entrance into the new life in Christ. To say that a man is baptized is to say that he has become a member of the Christian Church and has by his public confession become one with the people of God. The act of baptism is, therefore, in the words of Principal Davidson, "the whole experience that is properly described as initiation into the Christian society, as passing from darkness to light, from death to life, from flesh and sin to spirit and grace, as involving a complete break with the sinful past and a total commitment to Christ." [15] It is, therefore, a mistake to speak of baptized children "joining the Church" when they are received into communicant membership. They are already members of the Church and come to the Lord's Supper by the confirmation of their baptismal vows and the renewal of their engagement to be the Lord's. This initiation into membership implies admission, not merely into a local Church or denomination, but into membership in the Holy Catholic Church, the Church of Christ in all the world.

In the sacrament of Christian baptism there is always the use of water, and the spoken formula, " I baptize thee in the Name of the Father, and of the Son, and of the Holy Ghost." This act, and this alone, constitutes valid Christian baptism. In the ritual service, however, this sacramental act is preceded by what is called the " epiklesis," or the consecrating prayer in which the presence of the Holy Spirit is invoked. We may not understand or be united in our interpretation of how the blessing of the Holy Spirit attends the sacrament but we do know that apart from the presence of the Spirit of God no sacramental action takes place. Here the language of Calvin is unmistakable. The sacraments, he affirms, " only perform their office aright when they are accompanied by the Spirit, that internal Teacher, by whose energy alone our hearts are penetrated, our affections are moved, and an entrance is opened for the sacraments into our souls. If he be absent, the sacraments can produce no more effect upon our minds than the splendour of the sun on blind eyes, or the sound of a voice on deaf ears. I make such a distinction and distribution, therefore, between the Spirit and the sacraments, that I consider all the energy of operation as belonging to the Spirit, and the sacraments as mere instruments, which, without his agency, are vain and useless, but which, when he acts and exerts his power in the heart, are fraught with surprising efficacy." [16] If the question is pressed, " What, then, does the Holy Spirit do in the sacrament of baptism? " the answer is both negative and positive. Negatively, the Spirit does not change, alter, or influence the elements. Positively, the Spirit is present — in blessing, in every part of the Sacrament: the elements, the words of the institution, the act of consecration, the administration, and the reception by faith on the part of the believer. It is one act, and in that act there is the accompanying blessing of God.

If there is emphasis to be placed upon any single action within the unity of the sacramental act, it must be laid upon the faith of the recipient, and this fact is always recognized. Even the Orthodox Eastern Church, which holds to an *ex opere operato* view says in its ritual that the rite or " mystery " " conveys to the soul of a faithful man, the invisible grace of God." The tendency, however, in Churches which hold to the inherent virtue of the sacraments, when properly administered, is to regard them as conveying grace in and of themselves, even though the recipient be not " a faithful man." It was here the Reformers took their stand, upon firm ethical grounds, and constantly reiterated and repeated the doctrine that the sacrament had virtue only as it was accompanied by the faith of him who received it. " From this sacrament," says Calvin, " as from all others, we obtain nothing except what we receive by faith. If faith be wanting, it will be a testimony of our ingratitude, to render us guilty before God, because we have not believed the promise given in the sacrament; but as baptism is a sign of our confession, we ought to testify by it, that our confidence is in the mercy of God, and our purity in the remission of sins, which is obtained for us by Jesus Christ; and that we enter into the Church of God in order to live in the same harmony of faith and charity, of one mind with all the faithful." [17] Furthermore, as faith is the prerequisite to the reception of the grace of God in the sacrament, so the sacrament in turn confirms and increases the faith of the believer. The grace of the Holy Spirit accompanies the sacrament and leads into a deeper Christian experience.

V. Who Are to Be Baptized

BAPTISM in the New Testament is administered to believers and marks their entrance into the Christian faith and into fellowship with the people of God. The Church is the company of those who believe in Jesus. Baptist Churches, therefore, which say that baptism is for believers only, seem to have the New Testament on their side. The words which the First Gospel puts in the mouth of Jesus, and which belong at least to the time when the Gospel was written, call upon the followers of Jesus first to " make disciples of all the nations," and then to baptize them " into the name of the Father and of the Son and of the Holy Spirit." The first word of the Church at Pentecost was, " Repent ye, and be baptized." Always there is the voluntary and conscious acceptance of Christ. It is the believing Paul who is baptized. It is the faith of Cornelius that justifies baptism. It is the expressed belief of the jailer at Philippi that immediately assures baptism. " As many of you as were baptized into Christ did put on Christ." [1]

From whence, then, do the Christian Churches, both Catholic and Protestant, receive authority to practice the sacrament of baptism in the case of infants who cannot express conscious faith in the Lord Jesus Christ? The Baptist position has been stated categorically, that only " believer's baptism " was observed in apostolic times, and the Churches so believing number their membership in the millions. Their position is clearly set forth in the textbook *Systematic Theology*, by Charles Augustus Strong, which has guided the thinking of several generations of theological students. Dr. Strong, speaking for all Baptists, states unequivocally that the baptism of children is to be " rejected and reprehended." Those are strong words, but they express perfectly the attitude of those who adhere to believer's baptism only. " The proper subjects of baptism," he says, " are those who give credible evidence that they have been regenerated by the Holy Spirit." [2] He claims that the nature of the Church makes any other position untenable. " The church is a company of persons, whose union with one another presupposes and expresses a previous conscious and voluntary union of each with Jesus Christ." [3] He contends that infant baptism grew up in the Early Church because of the belief in baptismal regeneration. " The rise of infant baptism," he says, " is due to sacramental conceptions of Christianity so that all arguments in its favor from the writings of the first three centuries are equally arguments for baptismal regeneration." [4] The baptism of children, where parents become sponsors of the child in regard to faith, " unwarrantably confounds the personality of the child with that of the parent: practically ignores the necessity of the Holy Spirit's regenerating influences in the case of children of Christian parents: and presumes in such children a gracious state which facts conclusively show not to exist." [5] This is the position of those who assert that Christian baptism should be restricted to conscious believers and should not be administered to infants. Even recent writers on the subject, who maintain the Baptist position, feel so keenly on the subject that they suggest that the practice of infant baptism be surrendered in the interest of Church unity and the ecumenical Christian movement. A recent popular presentation of the Baptist position asserts that " if Congregational bodies would abandon infant baptism there would be a possibility of union, but Baptists maintain that their insistence upon believer's baptism as an essential Christian witness must be maintained." [6]

The fact that this position is held by a minority of Christians, while the great body of the Christian Church — Roman Catholic, Greek Catholic, and Protestant — administer the sacrament to infants, does not decide the issue, for it has often been true that the minority has been right; but it does call for explanation. If the Baptist position is right, how does it come about that from the very earliest time infant baptism has been administered? That it has been accepted is not a matter of dispute. It is a fact of history. Justin Martyr, writing not later than A.D. 150, mentions that there were in his time many in the Church who were then sixty or seventy years of age who had been disciples of Christ since childhood.[7] Irenaeus, a follower of Polycarp who was a disciple of John, said, " Christ came to save, through means of Himself, all who through Him are born again unto God, infants, and little children, and boys and youths, and old men." [8] Tertullian argued against baptism not only of infants but of children, which is evidence that such baptism was the accepted practice of his day. It certainly was not an innovation. Origen states that the custom had come down from apostolic times. Cyprian discussed with one Fidus the question whether a child should be baptized immediately or, as in the case of circumcision, on the eighth day, and took the position that the child should be baptized as soon as possible. By the third century infant baptism was obligatory in the North African Church, and Augustine, toward the end of the fourth century, wrote: " Therefore an infant, although he is not yet a believer in the sense of having that faith which includes the consenting will of those who exercise it, nevertheless becomes a believer through the sacrament of that faith. . . . The infant, though not yet possessing a faith helped by the understanding, is not obstructing faith by an antagonism of the understanding, and therefore receives with profit the sacrament of faith." [9] At an even earlier period Chrysostom said: " You see how many are the benefits of Baptism. And yet some think that the Heavenly grace consists only in forgiveness of sins: but I have reckoned up ten advantages of it. For this cause we baptize infants also, though they are not defiled with sin: that there may be superadded to them Holiness, Righteousness, Adoption, Inheritance, a Brotherhood with Christ, and to be made Members of him." [10] It is therefore no surprise that the official approval of the Church was given to the administration of baptism to infants by the Council of Carthage in A.D. 418, which affirmed that " whosoever denies that infants newly from their mother's womb should be baptized, or says that baptism is for remission of sins, but that they derive from Adam no original sin, which is removed by the laver of regeneration, whence the conclusion follows that in them the form of baptism for the remission of sins is to be understood as false and not true, let him be anathema." [11]

It can, of course, be contended that the Early Church was mistaken in its authorization of infant baptism. Those who oppose the custom say that the Early Church, or the so-called Fathers of the Church, possessed no authority to change the doctrine and teaching of the New Testament. They hold that since the New Testament is silent on the subject the sacrament of baptism should be confined to believers who have experienced the saving grace of God and who have received the gift of the Holy Spirit. Neither the Early Church nor the Church of today has the right to change the nature of the ordinance.

On what grounds and for what reason did the Early Church baptize infants and why has the main body of the Christian Church maintained its right to do so to the present day? If there were in the New Testament any definite statement to the effect that baptism should not be administered to little children, then we should be constrained to follow New Testament guidance. There is, however, no such prohibition and there is at the same time presumptive evidence that children were included in the covenant of grace and in the fellowship of the Christian Church. Paul goes so far as to say that " the unbelieving husband is sanctified in the wife, and the unbelieving wife is sanctified in the brother: else were your children unclean; but now are they holy." [12] There are repeated references in the New Testament to the baptism of whole families and households, and it is inconceivable that there were no little children in these homes. The family then, as now, was an organic unit and as a unit was received into community life. In speaking of Cornelius, the Roman centurion who was led into the Christian faith by a special visitation of Peter, it is stated that " the Holy Spirit fell on all them that heard the word." [13] It must have been a surprise to Peter himself to see the work of the Holy Spirit made manifest in the home of a Gentile, but immediately he said, " Can any man forbid the water, that these should not be baptized, who have received the Holy Spirit as well as we? And he commanded them to be baptized in the name of Jesus Christ." [14] That was a baptism that included all " kinsmen and near friends," and in all probability children. In like manner Lydia, the first Christian convert in Europe, was received into the fellowship of believers and " she was baptized, and her household." [15] It would be strange if no children were in such a household, and no statement to the contrary is made. Later when the keeper of the prison in Philippi was led into the Christian faith, Paul took him forthwith and he " was baptized, he and all his, immediately." [16] It was the confirmation of an act of faith on the part of the head of the house. In his first letter to the Church of Corinth, Paul states that he baptized " the household of Stephanas." [17] Certainly the language is unusual and points to a family unity which was and is characteristic of the followers of Christ. These are only a few among thousands of families who must have been welcomed into the Christian fellowship and who as families received baptism. In a land where children were looked upon as an expression of favor on the part of the Almighty, it would be strange if no little children were included in the " household." It would seem that even adults were also admitted to baptism because of the faith of the head of the household. These references, of course, give no positive assurance that in the New Testament Church the baptism of infants was observed, but it is pertinent to recognize the fact that the baptism of families and households is presumptive evidence that children were included.

The incorporation of children within the covenant of grace would be most natural for those who had been nurtured in the faith of the Old Testament covenant. Israel was a covenanted people. God pledged his promise and his presence, not merely to individuals, but to the believing community. The early Christians who were Jews understood what was meant by a covenant-keeping God. They understood what Peter was talking about in one of his first utterances: " Ye are the sons of the prophets, and of the covenant which God made with your fathers, saying unto Abraham, And in thy seed shall all the families of the earth be blessed." [18] What could be more natural than that all the meaning of that old covenant should be transferred by the early Christians to the new covenant, ratified for them by the work of Christ? If it is said that children cannot experience and express faith, the reply can be made that such a statement may prove too much. We would be compelled to say that infants dying in infancy since they cannot experience faith therefore cannot find salvation, and we are back again into that cold dark area of a limbo infantum. No evangelical Church is willing to take this position. Even the Baptist Churches themselves are eager to throw open the Kingdom of Heaven to all children dying in infancy and a Baptist Confession states that " we do believe that all little children dying in their infancy, viz. before they are capable to choose either good or evil, whether born of believing parents or unbelieving parents, shall be saved by the grace of God and merit of Christ their Redeemer, and the work of the Holy Ghost, and so being made members of the invisible Church shall enjoy life everlasting. For our Lord Jesus saith, Of such belongs the kingdom of heaven. Ergo, we conclude, that that opinion is false, which saith, that those little infants dying before baptism, are damned." [19]

The Christian Church is not, as has been asserted, " a group of individuals associating themselves together." The Church is a fellowship bound together in the faith of the Lord Jesus, and inspired and guided by the Holy Spirit. It would be hard to understand the exclusion of children from this fellowship. The relation of Jesus to children and his blessing bestowed on them has been always a powerful influence in the minds and

hearts of his followers. It was not children alone but also
infants who received the Saviour's blessing. Luke says: " They
were bringing unto him also their babes [τὰ βρέφη], that he
should touch them." [20]   Matthew and Mark speak of " little
children," παιδία.   Matthew adds a further lovely suggestion, " Then were there brought unto him little children, that
he should lay his hands on them, and pray." [21]   What words
regarding childhood can take their place beside those of Jesus:
" Suffer the little children, and forbid them not, to come unto
me: for to such belongeth the kingdom of heaven "? [22]   What
can his words mean if not that children, little children, belong
in his Kingdom?   " If I were to point to these roses, and say,
' Of such as these is the floral kingdom composed,' what would
you think of the good sense of a man, however wise he looked,
if he should go away and affirm that what I meant was, that
all flowers like roses were in the floral kingdom, but that roses
themselves were not?   Or if I were speaking of angels, and
said, ' Of such is the kingdom of heaven,' what sort of com-
mentator would he be who should argue from my words that
no angel was in that Kingdom, that they were all outside it?
And when our Lord, speaking of children, says: ' Of such is
the kingdom of God,' what can we think of those who argue
from His words that children themselves are not in God's
Kingdom? " [23]

The Christian home was the first Church, and it was inevitable that infant baptism should become the natural practice
of the early Christians.   This can be understood if it is remembered that the Church began as a distinctly missionary
enterprise.   The disciples, in response to the Lord's command,
went everywhere preaching the Gospel, making disciples, baptizing them in the name of the Lord Jesus.   The Acts outlines
their missionary program.   Beginning at Jerusalem, their ministry of evangelism took them through Judea into Samaria and
" unto the uttermost part of the earth." [24]   As the missionary
movement multiplied the number of converts, the question as
to who were to be baptized occasioned no difficulty.   Those

who expressed faith and repentance were baptized in the name
of the Lord Jesus. The question of the baptism of children
would become urgent as the second or third generation of
Christians were born into the Christian fellowship. As Christianity expanded and won whole households to the faith, it
was natural that the children of the first and second and third
generations were also admitted through baptism to the blessings of the new covenant. The Christian conception of the
Church as a fellowship, a *koinonia*, a family of God, a household of faith, would of necessity lead, as it still does, to the
inclusion, within the fellowship, of the children of believers.

The idea that the Christian Church is a community of believers together with their children is a position that should
be better understood than it is today. The Church has become
too individualistic and has failed to emphasize its solidarity
and social nature. No better statement of this neglected truth
has been made than is contained in Horace Bushnell's *Christian
Nurture*, published nearly one hundred years ago and still one
of the best treatises on Christian education. Dr. Bushnell
fought the charge of heresy because he contended for the rights
of children to grow up naturally into Christian faith and life.
He claimed this to be the true evangelism as against the current
revivalism which neglected the child and then sought to recover him when he reached maturity. In his epoch-making
book Bushnell maintained that " all society is organic — the
church, the state, the school, the family; and there is a spirit
in each of these organisms, peculiar to itself, and more or less
hostile, more or less favorable to religious character, and to
some extent, at least, sovereign over the individual man. A
very great share of the power in what is called a revival of
religion, is organic power; nor is it any the less divine on that
account. The child is only more within the power of organic
laws than we all are. We possess only a mixed individuality
all our life long. A pure, separate, individual man, living
wholly within, and from himself, is a mere fiction. No such
person ever existed, or ever can. I need not say that this view

of an organic connection of character subsisting between parent and child, lays a basis for nations of Christian education, far different from those which now prevail, under the cover of a merely fictitious and mischievous individualism." [25]

It was for this reason that the Reformers strove earnestly to have baptism administered in the Church in the presence of a worshiping congregation. In a real sense the Christian Church is the true sponsor of the child, and in receiving him into its fellowship it implicitly promises and pledges itself to see that the child is brought up in the Christian faith and within the Christian Church. When it seems wise to baptize a child in the home, or in some other place than the Christian sanctuary, care should be taken to see that baptism is recognized not as a private or priestly function. Baptism is not the act of the minister or of the parents, but is the act of God working in and through the Church ordinance. It is because this fact has been obscured that the sacrament of baptism has frequently been associated with superstition or magic, or has become a mere ritual of name-giving. To speak of the christening of a little child or of an adult is to ignore the authority of the Church. It is the Church that administers the sacrament, and anything that tends to separate this sacramental service from the life and worship of the Church robs it of its essential meaning. For this reason P. T. Forsyth, outstanding theologian of the Reformed tradition, writes with profound conviction. " It is the Church," he says, " that does the sacramental act. Nay, more, they are the acts of Christ really present by His Holy Spirit in the Church. It is Christ doing something through the Church as His body. It is only after these two higher senses are met that they are the acts of an individual. In the Community, individual administration is against its nature. Baptism is not primarily an act of the parent, nor of the child, but of the Church and of Christ in the Church. It is our individualism that has done most to ruin the sacrament of Baptism among us. We get a wrong answer because we do not put the right question. We ask, What good does Baptism do me or that child? Instead of, What is the active witness and service the Church renders to the active Word of Christ's Gospel in the Baptism of young or old? Baptism is not there primarily for the individual, nor for the family, but for the Church, to confess before God and man the Word of Regeneration." [26]

The acceptance of the obligations implied in infant baptism, on the part both of parents and of the Christian Church, would go far toward solving the problem of religious education of children and youth. Both the Christian home and the Christian Church stand convicted of failing to bring up children " in the nurture and admonition of the Lord." We are told that the past has produced a generation of illiterate Christians. There will be no improvement until baptismal obligations are understood and accepted. It is a disservice to " household religion " when the Church and the school give parents the impression that they have taken over the religious education of the child. The Magna Charta of Hebrew religion obtains also for Christians: " Hear, O Israel: Jehovah our God is one Jehovah: and thou shalt love Jehovah thy God with all thy heart, and with all thy soul, and with all thy might. And these words, which I command thee this day, shall be upon thy heart; and thou shalt teach them diligently unto thy children, and shalt talk of them when thou sittest in thy house, and when thou walkest by the way, and when thou liest down, and when thou risest up." [27] When parents realize that if they fail in keeping their solemn vows their child will lose what he ought to receive, then perhaps they will not seek to evade their obligations. And when the Church takes seriously its pledged sponsorship of the child, then it will provide an adequate teaching staff and an adequate program of religious education. It will not spend more money on a high-priced choir than it does in training children and youth in the Christian life, for it will do what Jesus did — take " a little child, and set him in the midst."

VI. The Administration of Baptism

IN THE administration of the sacrament of Christian baptism certain acts are involved. First of all, there is the use of water. The early Christian writers speak of pure water and living water. Since baptism symbolizes purification, common water, not holy water, is used, and the meaning and significance of the rite will depend somewhat on the mode of administration. In the second place, there is the prayer for the blessing of the Holy Spirit, commonly called the epiklesis. In this prayer the water is set apart from a common to a sacred use. We bless and " set apart " the elements of bread and wine in the Eucharist, and we follow the same ritual in the use of the water. The water is thereby not changed or rendered efficacious, save as a new sacredness attaches to the rite. There is, finally, the formula which has been used by the Early Church and all Churches, Catholic and Protestant, in all the centuries: " I baptize thee in the Name of the Father, and of the Son, and of the Holy Spirit." These three acts are, however, one. The sacramental act includes the use of water, the invocation of the Holy Spirit, and the words of the baptismal formula.

In times of emergency, however, even this simplicity has been further simplified and baptism has taken place without prayer. This is the mode when baptism is administered by a nurse, or doctor, or other layman in the absence of clergy, as in cases of approaching death or other necessity. The Roman Catholic and other Churches permit baptism to be thus administered, while among many Protestant Churches the right of administration rests solely with the ordained clergy. Calvin says: " It is not right for private persons to take upon themselves the administration of baptism; for this, as well as the administration of the Lord's supper, is a part of the public ministry of the Church. Christ never commanded women, or men in general, to baptize; he gave this charge to those whom he had appointed to be apostles." [1] When the question of emergency is raised, Calvin replies that baptism is not necessary to salvation and that infants are adopted as children of God and that baptism is administered to them as a seal not to give the covenant of grace validity but as the confirmation of that covenant. Calvin's position, though followed by the Reformed Church, has not had universal adherence. The Baptist Churches admit the validity of baptism by a layman as do also the Lutheran Churches. The Disciples of Christ make use of ordained elders or deacons. The Methodist Church, in remote missionary areas, permits baptism by an ordained layman, as does also the United Church of Canada. The Protestant Episcopal Church requires baptism by " a priest episcopally ordained," and this order is followed by the Greek Orthodox Church.

The question of the validity of administration was not raised by the Reformers. Tertullian, in his treatise *On Baptism,* deals with it, thus revealing the fact that it was discussed in the early centuries of the Church. He says: " The chief priest, who is the bishop, has the right of giving it; in the second place, the presbyters and deacons, yet not without the bishop's authority, on account of the honor of the Church. When this has been preserved, peace is preserved. Besides these, even laymen have the right; for what is equally received can be equally given. If there are no bishops, priests, or deacons, other disciples are called. The word of the Lord ought not to be hidden away by any. In like manner, also, baptism, which is equally God's property, can be administered by all; but how much more is the rule of reverence and modesty incumbent on laymen, since these things belong to their superiors, lest they assume to themselves the specific functions of the episcopate! " [2] The position of this eminent Church Father is embodied in the decree of the Roman Church, and, in answer to the question, " Who can confer Baptism in case of necessity? " the reply is: " In case of necessity anyone can confer Baptism without the ceremonies. If, however, a priest is present a deacon yields to him, a subdeacon to a deacon, a layman to a cleric, a woman to a man unless perhaps for modesty's sake it should prove more fitting for a woman to baptize than for a man, or if again it should prove that the woman knows the form and the method of baptizing better than the man." [3] On this subject we will be guided in our final judgment by our conception of the nature of the Church and the significance of baptism as a sacrament of the Church.

The history of the controversy regarding the mode of baptism need not be traced here. It can be followed in countless books and articles, which reflect bitter differences, thus holding back the ecumenical movement. Fortunately for the cause of the Christian religion, the movement toward co-operation and good understanding now rests on a firm foundation. Dr. George Truett, the foremost Baptist preacher of our generation, sometime ago stated the evangelical position in clear, strong words. " We hold," he said, " the immemorial position of Baptists that all true believers in Christ are saved, having been born again; and this without the intervention of preacher, priest, ordinance, sacrament or church. . . . We rejoice in our spiritual union with all who love the Lord Jesus. We hold them as brothers in the saving grace of Christ and heirs with us of life and immortality. We . . . maintain that the spiritual union of all believers is a reality. This spiritual union does not depend on organizations, or forms or rituals. It is deeper, higher, broader, and more stable than any or all organizations. We hold that all people who believe in Christ as their personal Saviour are our brothers in the common salvation, whether they be in the Catholic communion, or in a Protestant communion, or in any other communion, or in no communion." [4] These are healing and gracious words.

This does not mean that the Churches which hold to immersion as the only true mode of baptism have in any way modified their position. The Churches which practice baptism by immersion are strong and influential, and are too numerous to catalogue here. The complete list of such Churches in America may be found in the report of the United States Religious Census for 1936. This includes the various bodies, numbering about twenty, calling themselves Baptists, with an approximate membership of over 8,000,000; the Disciples of Christ, with over 1,000,000 members; and the Eastern Orthodox Churches, which practice both adult and infant baptism by threefold immersion and which admit both adults and infants to the sacrament of the Eucharist. These Eastern Orthodox Churches include the American Holy Orthodox Catholic Apostolic Eastern Church, and the Bulgarian, the Greek, the Rumanian, the Russian, the Serbian, the Syrian, the Ukrainian Orthodox Churches. Included in the immersionist group are the Church of the Brethren (Dunkers), the Church of God (Dunkers), the Advent Christian and the Seventh Day Adventist, the Church of God, the Plymouth Brethren, the Pentecostal Church, and the Church of Jesus Christ of Latter-day Saints (Mormon).

The position taken by these Churches is clear and easily understood. They contend that the New Testament sanctions no other mode, and consequently there is no authority in the teaching of Christ and the apostles for baptism by sprinkling or pouring. They rest their position largely upon the meaning of the word " to baptize," which we are told always signifies, " To immerse." Liddell and Scott define the word, " To dip in or under water." It is akin to the Latin *immergere*. Thayer gives the definition, " Literally to dip or dip repeatedly, to immerse, to submerge." It is asserted that " from the age of Greek literature down to its close, a period of nearly two thousand years, not an example has been found in which the word has any other meaning. There is no instance in which it signifies to make a partial application of water by affusion or sprinkling or to cleanse, to purify apart from the literal act of immersion as a means of cleansing or purifying." [5] Furthermore, they assert that the word and the New Testament practice both point to immersion. The word is used frequently

in connection with the Greek word *eis* which means " into."
Baptism took place where there was much water. The baptism of John took place at the Jordan. The people " were
baptized of him in the river Jordan." [6] " I indeed baptize
you in water." [7] " Jesus, when he was baptized, went up
straightway from the water." [8] In the record concerning the
ministry of John we have the statement, " John also was baptizing in Ænon near to Salim, because there was much water
there: and they came, and were baptized." [9] When we come
into the history of the ministry of the Apostolic Church similar expressions and implications are discovered. The Ethiopian
said to Philip, " Behold, here is water; what doth hinder me
to be baptized? " " And they both went down into the water,
both Philip and the eunuch; and he baptized him." [10] On the
whole this interpretation of the word " to baptize " is usually
conceded. Calvin, who denied the Baptist position, said:
" The very word baptize, however, signifies to immerse; and
it is certain that immersion was the practice of the ancient
Church." [11]

Moreover, the Baptists hold a strong position when they
point to the New Testament reference to baptism and to the
symbolic significance of the rite. In the New Testament there
are many references to baptism as a symbol of purification, of
cleansing, but there are also repeated references to the symbolism of dying to sin and rising again into newness of life.
In writing to the Christians at Rome, Paul says, " We were
buried therefore with him through baptism into death: that
like as Christ was raised from the dead through the glory of
the Father, so we also might walk in newness of life." [12] In
his letter to the Colossians he uses similar language. Christians
who had received Christ were " buried with him in baptism,
wherein ye were also raised with him through faith in the
working of God, who raised him from the dead." [13] In his
letter to the Church at Corinth, Paul speaks of the fathers'
passing under the cloud and through the sea, being " all baptized unto Moses in the cloud and in the sea." [14] The sym-

bolism is unmistakable and possesses a profound spiritual significance. The impressive words of Benjamin Jowett, master of Balliol, cannot be lightly set aside. " Imagine," he says, " not infants, but crowds of grown-up persons already changed in heart and feelings; their ' life hidden with Christ in God,' losing their personal consciousness in the laver of regeneration; rising again from its depths into the light of heaven, in communion with God and nature; met as they rose from the bath with the white raiment, which is ' the righteousness of the saints,' and ever after looking back on that moment as the instant of their new birth, of putting off of the old man, and the putting on of Christ. Baptism was to them the figure of death, burial, and resurrection all in one, the most apt expression of the greatest change that can pass upon man, like the sudden change into another life when we leave the body." [15]

The Churches that do not practice baptism exclusively by immersion would seem to be on the defensive. If immersion is the mode of administration in the New Testament, by what authority do Roman Catholics, Presbyterians, Methodists, Episcopalians, and others depart from it and practice baptism by sprinkling or by pouring? Furthermore, does not a change in the mode signify a change also in the meaning and significance of the rite? Is it possible that sprinkling or pouring can symbolize death unto sin and resurrection unto righteousness as is done by immersion? What, then, is the position of the Churches which do not follow the Baptist tradition?

It should be clearly kept in mind that the validity of baptism by immersion is universally recognized. Members entering the communion of evangelical Churches from Churches practicing immersion are not rebaptized. Their baptism is valid. Members, however, who enter the fellowship of Baptist Churches are rebaptized by immersion. There are Churches which, though holding to immersion, do, nonetheless, receive members from other evangelical Churches and do not insist on rebaptism, but they are irregular in their Church procedure. Churches which practice by sprinkling or

pouring do not deny but openly claim the validity of baptism
by immersion.   The Roman Catholic doctrine is that "Baptism can be validly given by immersion, infusion or aspersion." [16]   The Westminster Confession of Faith asserts that
" dipping of the person into the water is not necessary; but Baptism is rightly administered by pouring or sprinkling water
upon the person." [17]

Those Christian Churches which, while admitting that the
word " to baptize " usually means " to immerse," hold that it
does not always do so.   The spiritual insight and fine scholarship of Bishop Moule, for example, constrained him to say:
" Beyond doubt the *ideal* of Baptism was immersion.   There
is no proof however that actual immersion was ever a vital
necessity to the rite; the symbolical washing somehow would
probably be enough for signification.   The verb ' baptize ' is
certainly not conclusive." [18]   The word " to baptize," βα-
πτίζειν, while ordinarily translated " to immerse," is also used
in the sense of cleansing, washing, purification.   In the Gospel
of Mark we read: " For the Pharisees, and all the Jews, except
they wash their hands diligently, eat not, holding the tradition of the elders; and when they come from the market-
place, except they bathe themselves, they eat not; and many
other things there are, which they have received to hold, washings of cups, and pots, and brasen vessels." [19]   In these verses
we have the word βαπτίσωνται translated " bathe themselves,"
and the word βαπτισμούς translated " washings."   The mar-
gin of the Revised Version suggests that the Greek word is
" baptize."   Furthermore, in this connection, the two important manuscripts, the Sinaiticus and the Vaticanus, instead
of the word βαπτίσωνται give the word ραντίσωνται, which
is rightly translated " sprinkle."   In the Gospel of Luke we
have the words, " When the Pharisee saw it, he marvelled that
he had not first bathed himself before dinner." [20]   Here the
word for " bathed " is ἐβαπτίσθη.   It would be difficult indeed to think of such washings, bathings, purifications, as im-
plying necessarily immersion.   In The Epistle to the Hebrews

we find the word "baptize" used in the sense of "wash." There are two examples. In ch. 9:10 we read, "Meats and drinks and divers washings." The word for "washings" is βαπτισμοῖς. Again in v. 19 we have the statement, "He took the blood of the calves and the goats, with water and scarlet wool and hyssop, and sprinkled both the book itself and all the people." Here the word used for "sprinkled" is ἐρράντισε, which has the same significance as the word βαπτισμοῖς in the verse already quoted. It would seem, therefore, that sometimes the words "baptize" and "sprinkle" were used interchangeably.

Furthermore, within the area of the period of the Apostolic Church, baptism by sprinkling or pouring was in practice. Not later than the first half of the second century, in the *Didache* or "Teaching of the Twelve" already referred to, there occur these significant instructions, which have particular importance in this connection: "Concerning baptism, thus shall ye baptize. Having first recited all these things, baptize in the name of the Father and of the Son and of the Holy Spirit in living [i.e., running] water. But if thou hast not living water, then Baptize in any other water; and if thou art not able in cold, in warm. But if thou hast neither, pour water upon the head thrice in the name of the Father and of the Son and of the Holy Spirit. But before baptism let him that baptizeth and him that is baptized fast, and any others also who are able; and thou shalt order him that is baptized to fast a day or two before." [21] This evidence does not stand alone. Cyprian (A.D. 258) states that in the case of illness baptism may be administered by pouring. It would seem that immersion was not a *sine qua non* for the administering of the rite of baptism. There is further evidence to be found in the catacombs, and in early art preserved for us, that baptism was administered by aspersion or pouring, the person to be baptized standing in the water and the water being lifted by the hand or by the use of a shell. Not only is this testimony borne as to the mode of baptism, but there are also inscriptions stating that children and infants had been baptized. A competent authority on the catacombs says: " In the Chambers of the Sacraments there is also a scene depicting real Baptism by immersion and aspersion. One person stands with part of the body immersed, another pours water on him. The picture is completed by another close by representing the paralytic in the pool. The same allusion is found on a fresco of the so-called region of St. Sorter where the disciples of the Good Shepherd pour water on the heads of the sheep." [22]

The expanding influence of the Church called for many changes in Church worship and order. Far removed from the Jordan Valley and its associations groups of Christians met in homes, in synagogues, and, in course of time, in their own Churches and chapels. The sense of freedom belonged to them. The battle which Paul waged against a restrictive Judaism had been won. At the critical council held at Jerusalem a decision was reached that freed the Christian faith from bondage to Jewish forms and ceremonies. Speaking for the council, James, the head of the Church at Jerusalem, said, " It seemed good to the Holy Spirit, and to us, to lay upon you no greater burden than these necessary things." [23] The decision was that no unnecessary hindrances should be put in the way of any man's becoming a Christian, be he Jew or Gentile.

It was this latter position which the Reformers took. They felt free to modify the rituals of both baptism and the Lord's Supper, provided they remained true to the essential nature of the sacraments. John Calvin, with his accustomed freedom from the bondage to the letter, said, " Whether the person who is baptized be wholly immersed, and whether thrice or once, or whether water be only poured or sprinkled upon him, is of no importance; Churches ought to be left at liberty, in this respect, to act according to the difference of countries." [24] This was the position taken by the eminent Church historian, Philip Schaff: " It is a pedantic literalism to limit the operation of the Holy Ghost by the quantity or quality of the water." [25]

Christianity is no longer confined within the limits of a warm climate, where bathing in the open air is customary. Christianity has reached out unto the ends of the earth. It is in Alaska and Labrador, in prisons and reformatories, in concentration camps and hospitals, on board ships and in wayside chapels, and it is adapted and adaptable to all situations. "For freedom did Christ set us free." [26] It is not likely that the missionaries who traveled over sea and land, forming Christian communities, should feel bound, when conditions and environments changed, to abide by external forms. They did not do so in regard to the celebration of the Lord's Supper. It had been first observed in the evening, in an upper room, by a group of men who reclined as they partook of the Supper. It was celebrated in the Early Church in connection with the evening meal, following the agape, or love feast. These details are important if we are bound to follow in every detail the customs of the New Testament Church. They are unimportant in the light of the true purpose and meaning of the Eucharist. We do not feel obligated to use the kind of bread or wine which Jesus used. In all these situations we are free. There are many customs having New Testament sanction which the Church has surrendered. The "holy kiss," which was commended and in use, in due time passed away, and we would not think of reviving it. The custom of foot washing has not received Church recognition save in limited circles. In like manner, we properly celebrate the sacrament of baptism when water is used, irrespective of the quantity, and when the words, "In the Name of the Father, and of the Son, and of the Holy Spirit," are spoken. To affirm that we must follow in detail customs which were suitable at a particular time and in a particular country is to bind the Christian conscience to unnecessary externals.

VII. The Sacrament of the Lord's Supper

ONE of the marks of a sacrament is that it is instituted by our Lord Jesus Christ. What we do is done at his command. Each of the Gospels, and also Paul, rests the authority for the celebration of the Lord's Supper in Christ himself. He instituted the Sacrament. He interpreted it. He commanded his followers to continue its observance " till he come." It will be best, therefore, to set down the New Testament passages which contain all that we really need as to the meaning and significance of this holy ordinance. It will not be necessary here to follow critically the chronological order in which they appeared.

We begin with the Gospels. Matthew states:

" As they were eating, Jesus took bread, and blessed, and brake it; and he gave to the disciples, and said, Take, eat; this is my body. And he took a cup, and gave thanks, and gave to them, saying, Drink ye all of it; for this is my blood of the covenant, which is poured out for many unto remission of sins. But I say unto you, I shall not drink henceforth of this fruit of the vine, until that day when I drink it new with you in my Father's kingdom." (Ch. 26: 26–29.)

In like manner Mark, on whom the other Synoptic Gospels depend, says:

" As they were eating, he took bread, and when he had blessed, he brake it, and gave to them, and said, Take ye: this is my body. And he took a cup, and when he had given thanks, he gave to them: and they all drank of it. And he said unto them, This is my blood of the covenant, which is poured out for many." (Ch. 14: 22–24.)

In Luke's Gospel the account is slightly different — the giving of the cup precedes the giving of the bread:

" He received a cup, and when he had given thanks, he said, Take this, and divide it among yourselves: for I say unto you, I shall not drink from henceforth of the fruit of the vine, until the kingdom of God shall come. And he took bread, and when he had given thanks, he brake it, and gave to them, saying, This is my body which is given for you: this do in remembrance of me. And the cup in like manner after supper, saying, This cup is the new covenant in my blood, even that which is poured out for you." (Ch. 22:17–20.)

There are two important passages in Paul's First Epistle to the Corinthians, which preceded in time those given in the Gospels. The first contains Paul's own interpretation of the Sacrament:

" The cup of blessing which we bless, is it not a communion of the blood of Christ? The bread which we break, is it not a communion of the body of Christ? seeing that we, who are many, are one bread, one body: for we all partake of the one bread." (Ch. 10:16, 17.)

The more familiar passage, used in the sacramental ritual, contains, as Paul asserts, the instructions of Jesus himself:

" I received of the Lord that which also I delivered unto you, that the Lord Jesus in the night in which he was betrayed took bread; and when he had given thanks, he brake it, and said, This is my body, which is for you: this do in remembrance of me. In like manner also the cup, after supper, saying, This cup is the new covenant in my blood: this do, as often as ye drink it, in remembrance of me. For as often as ye eat this bread, and drink the cup, ye proclaim the Lord's death till he come." (I Cor. 11:23–26.)

In addition to these references it is necessary to include the sacramental passage in John's Gospel. In this Gospel there is no reference to the institution of the sacramental ordinance of the Lord's Supper. Many reasons are given for this omission, none of them very cogent. It is, however, pointed out that the sixth chapter, containing the miracle of the feeding of the five thousand and the consequent narrative concerning the Bread of Life, is essentially sacramental. In this narrative these striking verses appear:

" I am the living bread which came down out of heaven: if any man eat of this bread, he shall live for ever: yea and the bread which I will give is my flesh, for the life of the world.

" The Jews therefore strove one with another, saying, How can this man give us his flesh to eat? Jesus therefore said unto them, Verily, verily, I say unto you, Except ye eat the flesh of the Son of man and drink his blood, ye have not life in yourselves. He that eateth my flesh and drinketh my blood hath eternal life; and I will raise him up at the last day. For my flesh is meat indeed, and my blood is drink indeed. He that eateth my flesh and drinketh my blood abideth in me, and I in him. As the living Father sent me, and I live because of the Father; so he that eateth me, he also shall live because of me. This is the bread which came down out of heaven: not as the fathers ate, and died; he that eateth this bread shall live forever." (Ch. 6:51–58.)

The language is certainly sacramental. The words mean something other than they say. Jesus is using sacrificial language. It is the language of symbolism. " The ' flesh ' and ' blood ' represent in vivid, realistic manner Jesus Himself in His essential, and human, spirit of unique faith and of perfect obedience — which faith and obedience were supremely manifest in the Cross. There He gave His ' flesh ' and ' blood '; that is, there He dedicated His whole unique human self to God and to His fellows. To eat His flesh and to drink His blood is, therefore, to partake of His essential spirit." [1] Concerning the language, Frederick D. Maurice said that if he were asked if the reference here is to the Eucharist itself, he would have to say, " No," but if asked where the true meaning of the Eucharist could be learned he would say, " Nowhere so well as here."

It will be noticed that the words, " My blood of the covenant," " The new covenant in my blood," " A communion of the blood of Christ," repeat themselves in the Synoptic Gospels and in First Corinthians, and that the Fourth Gospel uses similar language: " He that eateth my flesh and drinketh my blood." It is language strange to us, but familiar to those who knew intimately the language and ritual of the Old Testament. The Old Testament set forth an old covenant, the covenant of the Law, which was sealed with blood. This covenant, however, had failed. God had done for man what he could, but man broke from his covenant relations through failure to keep perfectly the law of God. What man needed was not a new law but a new heart. The prophets saw this and spoke of it. " Behold, the days come, saith Jehovah, that I will make a new covenant with the house of Israel, and with the house of Judah: not according to the covenant that I made with their fathers in the day that I took them by the hand to bring them out of the land of Egypt; which my covenant they brake, although I was a husband unto them, saith Jehovah. But this is the covenant that I will make with the house of Israel after those days, saith Jehovah: I will put my law in their inward parts, and in their heart will I write it; and I will be their God, and they shall be my people." [2] This promise was fulfilled in Christ, who became " the mediator of the new covenant." The meaning is clearly expressed in The Epistle to the Hebrews, which sets forth the Gospel in " covenant " language. The argument is to the effect that the old covenant was disannulled because of its weakness and unprofitableness. The Law made nothing perfect. It was a failure. Therefore God " brought in " a better hope through Jesus who became " the surety of a better covenant " and is now " able to save to the uttermost them that draw near unto God through him." [3] The language is Old Testament language, but it means what the New Testament calls, " The gospel of the grace of God."

Furthermore, since the old covenant was sealed or certified to by blood, that is, by sacrifice, the writer to the Hebrews says: " Even the first covenant hath not been dedicated without blood. For when every commandment had been spoken by Moses unto all the people according to the law, he took the blood of the calves and the goats, with water and scarlet wool and hyssop, and sprinkled both the book itself and all the people, saying, This is the blood of the covenant which God commanded to you-ward." [4] In like manner the new covenant of grace is ratified, not by the blood of animals, but by the blood of Christ. " For if the blood of goats and bulls, and the ashes of a heifer sprinkling them that have been defiled, sanctify unto the cleanness of the flesh: how much more shall the blood of Christ, who through the eternal Spirit offered himself without blemish unto God, cleanse your conscience from dead works to serve the living God? And for this cause he is the mediator of a new covenant." [5] It is this language which repeats itself in the institution of the Lord's Supper. His atoning sacrifice is remembered as " the new covenant in my blood." We may not speak of " the blood of Christ " as our fathers did or as the great hymns of the Church still do. We prefer the language of Ignatius: " Do ye therefore arm yourselves with gentleness and be renewed in faith, which is the flesh of the Lord and *in love which is the blood of Jesus Christ.*" The emphasis is upon atonement by means of life. " The life is in the blood." When we say we are saved by the blood of Christ, we mean that we are saved by the living Christ who was crucified. This is the message of the Gospel, and this is the message of the Sacrament of the Lord's Supper.

The significance of the Sacrament centers upon the nature of the sacrifice commemorated in the Sacrament. When Jesus said, " This is my body," " This is my blood," what did he mean? When all the interpretations that have awakened faith and raised controversies have been examined, the one central question which must be answered is this: If the Sacrament is a sacrifice, what is the nature of the sacrifice? Is the sacrifice expiatory, that is, a repetition of the sacrifice of our Lord Jesus on Calvary, or is it a memorial of a sacrifice offered once and for all? Is Calvary repeated every time the Sacrament is celebrated? Is Christ crucified again at every Communion? In his drama, *Emperor and Galilean,* Ibsen makes Julian the Apostate say: " Behold there came a procession by me on the strange earth where I stood. There were soldiers and judges and executioners at the head of it, and weeping women followed. And lo, in the midst of the slow-moving array was the Galilean, alive and bearing a cross on his back. Then I called to him

and said, ' Whither away, Galilean? '   And he turned his face
to me and smiled, nodded slowly and said, ' To the place of the
skull.'   Where is he now?   What if that at Golgotha, near
Jerusalem, was but a wayside matter, a thing done as it were in
passing!   What if he goes on and on, and suffers and dies, and
conquers, again and again, from world to world! "   Is that,
then, the truth?   Is Jesus crucified again and again, not in
other worlds but in every Sacrament where his body is again
broken and his blood shed?

It is the teaching of a large section of Christendom, represented by the Roman and Greek Catholic Churches, that the
Lord's Supper is a veritable sacrifice, the offering upon the
altar of the body and blood of Christ.   The drama of the crucifixion is re-enacted.   At every Mass, Christ is again crucified
and openly exhibited.   The Host, the dying Victim, is lifted
up in the sight of the people.   This being so, it is possible to
" reserve " the transubstantiated elements in the sanctuary
and before them, as in his presence, to bow in adoration and
praise.   The power to perform this miracle is lodged in the
bishops and priests, the successors of the apostles, to whom
such power was committed.   The Church, through its clergy,
has " the power to produce the actual living Christ upon the
altar," according to Cardinal Vaughan.   In the period immediately following the Reformation, the Roman Church formulated its faith, and, in language difficult to follow, the teaching
has been set forth: " The Catholic Church, then, firmly believes,
and openly professes that in this Sacrament, the words of consecration accomplish three things; first, that the true and real
body of Christ, the same that was born of the Virgin, and is
now seated at the right hand of the Father in heaven, is rendered present in the Holy Eucharist; secondly, that however
repugnant it may appear to the dictate of the senses, no substance of the elements remains in the Sacrament; and thirdly, a
natural consequence from the two preceding, and one which
the words of consecration also express, that the accidents which
present themselves to the eyes, or other senses, exist in a won-

derful and ineffable manner without a subject. The accidents of bread and wine we see; but they inhere in no substance, and exist independently of any. The substance of the bread and wine is so changed into the body and blood of our Lord, that they, altogether, cease to be the substance of bread and wine." [6]

This interpretation is metaphysical and therefore is difficult to state in simple language. It is frequently stated that in the sacrifice of the Mass the bread and the wine become the physical body and blood of our Lord. This is the popular conception and is so interpreted by many, but it does not truly represent the Catholic position. Perhaps the situation may be clarified by an illustration taken from the life of one of Scotland's greatest preachers, Dr. Alexander Whyte, of Edinburgh. Dr. Whyte had a sincere admiration for Cardinal Newman and sent him his *Commentary on The Shorter Catechism*. In that handbook Dr. Whyte, in commenting upon the words, "Not after a corporal and carnal manner, but by faith, made partakers of his body and blood," said: "This is directed against the Popish doctrine of transubstantiation. According to that doctrine the bread and wine are changed into the very flesh and blood of Christ, so that all communicants literally and physically eat the flesh and drink the blood of Christ." [7] Cardinal Newman was not satisfied with this statement, and wrote a most interesting letter: " December 15, 1883. My dear Dr. Whyte — I thank you for your Commentary which you have sent me. It has interested me greatly: it rejoices me to meet with so much in it which I can sympathise and concur in, and I thank you heartily for the kind references you make to me in the course of it and for the words you have written in its first page. But it pains me that so large a heart as yours should so little enter into the teaching of the Catholic Church, let alone agreeing to it. Thus you say that we consider that we *physically* eat our Lord's flesh and drink His blood in the Holy Eucharist. It might quite as truly be said that in John vi, our Lord speaks of ' eating His flesh and drinking His blood ' physically as that we so speak.

We consider the *substance* of His body and blood to be in the
Sacrament, and thereby to be given to us, and you truly say
(p. 17), speaking of the Holy Trinity, that the ' substance ' is
that ' awful mysterious essence of which the qualities are *not*
extension, or colour, or figure,' etc., that is, ' physically,' but
that unknown reality to which sensible qualities attach themselves and belong, without being *it*. Excuse this outbreak of
controversy, and believe me to be, Most truly yours, John
Card. H. Newman." [8] In the second edition of the *Commentary,* Dr. Whyte substituted for his former statement these
words: " According to this doctrine, the substance of the bread
and wine is converted into the substance of the very flesh and
blood of Christ, so that all communicants literally and substantially partake of His flesh and blood." [9] The Catholic position metaphysically expressed by Cardinal Newman is the
official teaching of the Roman Church and is concurred in by
the Eastern Orthodox Church.

The Churches of evangelical Protestantism repudiate this
position. They hold to the teaching that the Sacrament does
celebrate the sacrifice of Christ, but teach that it is a memorial
sacrifice, a commemorative sacrifice. The sacrifice of Christ
on Calvary can never be repeated. The writer of The Epistle
to the Hebrews is emphatic concerning the finished work of
Christ, and points out how the sacrifice of Christ differs from
the repetitious sacrifices of the Old Testament. Christ has
obtained " eternal " redemption. The emphasis is upon the
finished work of Christ. " Christ entered not into a holy
place made with hands, like in pattern to the true; but into
heaven itself, now to appear before the face of God for us: nor
yet that he should offer himself often, as the high priest enter-
eth into the holy place year by year with blood not his own;
else must he often have suffered since the foundation of the
world: but now once at the end of the ages hath he been manifested to put away sin by the sacrifice of himself." [10] He was
" once offered." In the language of Dr. Wotherspoon, " The
sacrificial in the Sacrament then is that in it Christ is set forth

in the merit of His sacrifice on earth, as once crucified and now risen and ascended to appear in the presence of God for us. His death is shown, and His life. The act of Atonement is represented, as Christ represents it in His own person. It is a memorial, a witness, not a memory — a memorial of Him as He is and a union with Him as He acts. On our side of the veil and seen as we see ourselves acting, it is that, standing before God and in the worship of God, we show the Lord's Death as presently prevailing for our acceptance and as our plea for all God's mercy; and in unity with Christ's self-offering to the Father, we ourselves are offered." [11] It is this teaching that is enshrined in the documents that express the Reformed faith. "As the body and blood of Christ are not corporally or carnally present in, with, or under the bread and wine in the Lord's Supper; and yet are spiritually present to the faith of the receiver, no less truly and really than the elements themselves are to their outward senses; so they that worthily communicate in the Sacrament of the Lord's Supper, do therein feed upon the body and blood of Christ, not after a corporal or carnal, but in a spiritual manner; yet truly and really, while by faith they receive and apply unto themselves Christ crucified, and all the benefits of his death." [12] This position, while difficult to define in terms of the real presence of Christ in the Sacrament, nevertheless places the emphasis upon the faith by which we are able to perceive Christ's presence in the Sacrament. When we approach the holy table, it is to meet him who is the Host. We respond to his invitation. In the Sacrament we find him, as countless multitudes have found him, ministering to our spiritual need. Before we say, " I come," he says, " This is my body which is *given* for you."

It is in this sense we experience the Real Presence. The Real Presence is not discovered in the elements but in Him of whom the elements speak. How this takes place we do not know. We can say with Calvin, " I shall not be ashamed to acknowledge, that it is a mystery too sublime for me to be able to express, or even to comprehend; and, to be still more explicit,

I rather experience it, than understand it." [13]   When we say that Christ is present in the Sacrament, we assert that in the entire ordinance — in the words of the institution, which are his words; in the act of breaking the bread and pouring out of the wine; in the act of receiving by faith what is blessed in his name; in the action of the Holy Spirit in making everything embodied in the Sacrament efficacious — in all that is said and done Christ manifests himself to the believer.

VIII. The Celebration of Holy Communion

THE sacrament of the Lord's Supper has one meaning and one message. It commemorates the eternal sacrifice of Christ for us and for our salvation. At the same time, it holds in its keeping all the benefits of the new covenant. It presents to us Christ, and with Christ we receive from his hands what he has to give. These blessings and benefits are suggested by the various names by which this sacred ordinance is called.

It is called the *Passover*. Paul says, " Our passover also hath been sacrificed, even Christ." Therefore, he says, " Let us keep the feast, not with old leaven, neither with the leaven of malice and wickedness, but with the unleavened bread of sincerity and truth." [1] The Christian life is to be a festival of freedom, not from Egyptian bondage, but from the bondage of sin. The new Israel had passed from death unto life under the new covenant of grace. The old gave place to the new. All that was implied in the Jewish observance of the Passover was subordinated to higher values by Jesus. The slain lamb, the symbol of sacrifice, the partaking of the prepared feast, the sealing of the covenant promises to the people of God, were all taken up and symbolized in the Sacrament.

It is called the *Sacrament*. The word *sacramentum* had reference to the oath Roman soldiers took to the emperor. The first use of the word in a Christian sense is found in the letter of Pliny the Younger to the Emperor Trajan (A.D. 109). Pliny was honestly perplexed about how to deal with Christians who refused to worship at the shrine of the emperor, and in his letter to Trajan he speaks about the customs of the Christians in the Province of Bithynia. He says they were accustomed " to assemble on a fixed day before daybreak and sing antiphonally a hymn to Christ as a god; and that they *bound themselves with an oath* not for any crime, but to commit neither theft, nor robbery, nor adultery, not to break their word and not to deny a deposit when demanded; after these things were done, it was their custom to depart and meet together again to take food, but ordinary and harmless food." [2] In the phrase, " Bound themselves with an oath," is embedded the Latin word for sacrament. The word found its way into the Vulgate, the Latin version of the Bible, but in this case it was used to translate the word " mystery." The sacraments in the Roman Church are called " mysteries," but in the New Testament the word "mystery " is not so used. A mystery is something that has been revealed. " Behold, I tell you a mystery." In this sense a sacrament is indeed a mystery, for it is a revelation. It seeks to make clear the meaning and message of the cross of Christ.

It is called the *Lord's Supper*. The name had become familiar in the Early Church. Paul uses the words, " The Lord's supper," [3] and also, " The table of the Lord." [4] It is Christ himself who welcomes us to his table. He is the Host. We are the invited guests. He himself is the Food, and it is he who says, " Take, eat." He is the Priest and the Saving Sacrifice. " Once at the end of the ages hath he been manifested to put away sin by the sacrifice of himself." [5] The Lord's Supper was an evening meal instituted on the night he was betrayed, and it continued to be an evening meal. The custom of early Communion, however, has now become common in many Churches. The Roman Church, believing in the miracle of transubstantiation, demands that the people " approach the Holy Eucharist fasting," [6] in order that common food may not mingle with the very body and blood of Christ. Where this doctrine is held, early Mass is exalted, and the simplicity of the Lord's Supper is apt to be obscured.

It is called the *Communion*. The word is part of the sacramental ritual. " The cup of blessing which we bless, is it not a communion of the blood of Christ? The bread which we break, is it not a communion of the body of Christ? " [7]   The word is the Greek *koinonia* and it also occurs elsewhere in such words as fellowship, partaker, common. The Holy Communion is the sacred act of Christian fellowship, the bond of the members of the beloved society with each other and with their Saviour. What a world-wide fellowship it is and ought to be! And what a tragedy that it has often been the cause of separation and controversy! Herein is placed an inescapable obligation on every Christian that this act of Holy Communion become again, as it was in the Apostolic Church, a bond of union and a seal of Christian consecration to a common Lord.

It is called the *Eucharist*. The word appears in connection with the words of institution: " He took a cup, and gave thanks "; [8] " He took a cup, and when he had given thanks." [9] The Eucharist means the " thanksgiving." The prayer of thanksgiving is always part of the ritual of the Sacrament. Perhaps it would add to the immediate quickening of interest in the Sacrament if this note of triumph were sounded more constantly in our Communion meditation and our hymns, for the service is meant to speak to us of the victory through sacrifice of Him who in the Sacrament offers himself to us.

It is called the *Mass*. Protestantism has discarded the name, although Luther made frequent use of it. The first Prayer Book of Edward VI used the words, " The Supper of the Lord and Holy Communion, commonly called the Masse." The word is not found in the New Testament and did not make its appearance until the beginning of the seventh century. It comes from the Latin *mittere*, to send away or to dismiss. When the Eucharist was celebrated in the Early Church those who were not communicants were dismissed with the words, " *Ite, missa est.*" Gradually, however, the word was identified with the Roman interpretation of the Sacrament but was repudiated by the Protestant Church. The Thirty-first of the *Articles of Religion* says: " The sacrifices of Masses, in the which it was commonly said, that the Priest did offer Christ for the quick and the dead, to have remission of pain or guilt, were blasphemous fables, and dangerous deceits." In accordance with the canons of the Council of Trent, the priest of the Roman Church takes this vow: " I profess that in the Mass is offered a true, proper, and propitiatory sacrifice for the living and the dead, and that in the most holy Sacrament of the Eucharist, there is truly, really, and in substance, the body and blood, together with the soul and divinity, of our Lord Jesus Christ, and that there does take place a conversion of the entire substance of the wine into the blood, which conversion the Catholic Church doth call transubstantiation. I admit that under one or the other kinds alone the entire and whole Sacrament is received." [10]

The elaborate ceremony of the Mass is far removed from the simplicity of the Gospel. There is no doubt that it is a supreme drama. Anyone who sees the pageantry of a Eucharistic Congress, or even a High Mass in a great cathedral, must be impressed by the amazing spectacle. It re-enacts the sacrifice of Christ. The elements are lifted as the ritual prayer begins: " Receive, O Holy Father, this unspotted Host." The congregation kneels in silence. A portion of the bread is placed in the tabernacle to be worshiped and adored. This is the " reservation " of the Sacrament, and it is to this the people kneel in adoration.

The celebration of the Holy Communion, therefore, depends on the interpretation that is placed upon it. If it is a Mass, the celebration will be ritualistic and elaborate. If it is the Lord's Supper, it can be exceedingly simple. If it is a sacrifice offered on an altar, it will mean one thing. If it is served to those gathered around the Lord's table, it will signify something else. Of course the word " altar " may be used in a general sense, as the table used in the observance of the Sacrament, but in the technical sense an altar is the repository of a sacrifice. The table is a place around which the family of God gathers to commemorate the one and sufficient sacrifice of Christ. The table of the Reformed Church has a chair behind it where the

minister presides and administers the Sacrament. He faces
the people. The altar is the place before which the priest
kneels as he offers sacrifice. It is interesting to note, in this
connection, that Dr. Walter Lowrie, in his book on the Liturgy,
states that in all the early basilicas the minister faced the people. " It is the Holy Table which symbolizes the sacramental
unity of the Church. Accordingly it is appropriate that the
Church should gather around this table." [11]

It has been already pointed out that the Sacrament was the
norm of early Christian worship and that from the beginning
there has been a common framework within which the celebration of Holy Communion moved. This being the case,
there can be no excuse for carelessness or experimentation in
the administration of the Sacrament. The most thoughtful
and prayerful preparation should be made by both the minister and his people. The service may be, as in the Roman and
Greek communions, enshrined in richness of symbolism and
in choice language, or it may be as simple as it must have been
in the upper room; but always and everywhere it should be
administered with dignity and grace, and as far as possible in
silence, so that the message of the Sacrament itself may be
heard. It should be celebrated without hurry and without
distraction — for let it be remembered that in the service it is
God who is the actor, the great doer, the divine giver.

The ritual or order for the celebration of the Communion
should be a complete unity, with no preliminary service and
nothing partaking of the nature of a postlude. The whole
service from beginning to end should be directed to one central theme. It should not be an appendage to a regular
Church service which carries no thought of the Sacrament.
It should not be celebrated after the worship service has been
concluded. The whole service should form a part of the order
of celebration, so that, from the call to prayer to the benedic-
tion, everything will conform to the sacramental thought and
action. The hymns chosen, the anthems selected, the Scripture read, the sermon preached, should form a complete whole.

This does not mean that there is no freedom or liberty in the choice of hymns, Scripture, and sermon. It means that everything should minister to the due observance of the rite itself. If, for example, the sermon or Communion meditation has no relation to the cross of Christ, his death and resurrection, then it has no place in such a service. The message of the minister should be the same message as that of the Sacrament, and the eyes of the minister and of his people should be upon the cross, or rather upon him who suffered and triumphed there.

The manner of celebrating the Holy Communion varies in different Churches. There are differences even in the same denomination. Sometimes, as in the Episcopal Communion, the people come forward in a group and, kneeling before the holy table, are served the bread and the wine by the officiating minister. Retiring to their pews, they are followed by another group, and this order is continued until all have partaken. When the elements are administered, the minister in each case uses words such as: " The Body of our Lord Jesus Christ, which was given for thee, preserve thy body and soul unto everlasting life. Take and eat this in remembrance that Christ died for thee, and feed on him in thy heart by faith, with thanksgiving." [12] In administering the wine he says: " The Blood of our Lord Jesus Christ, which was shed for thee, preserve thy body and soul unto everlasting life. Drink this in remembrance that Christ's Blood was shed for thee, and be thankful." [13] It is an impressive order and emphasizes the fact that the soul is alone with God. God speaks and acts in behalf of each communicant.

In Reformed Churches the minister is assisted by elders or deacons, the congregation remaining in their pews. When this order is followed particular preparation is necessary so that there may be no confusion during the celebration. The minister and the elders should carefully study the order in use, and should rehearse the service in private so that each one may know his assigned place. There should be no distractions or innovations, and experiments should be avoided. The elders will appreciate being taught and guided in this matter, and the minister should take no liberties with the order for the celebration. In this way the congregation will know what to expect and will not be distracted by anything that is done or said, either in private or in public. All preparations for uncovering and covering the elements should be made. The manner of distribution should be carefully arranged. It is a service of sacramental silence in which the voice of God is heard. It is a time of self-examination, self-discipline, and personal commitment. A personal prayer may be printed in the bulletin, or memorized in confirmation classes or at the preparatory service. The prayer from the Liturgy of St. James may be most helpful: " O God, who by the life and death and rising again of Thy dear Son hast consecrated for us a new and living way into the holiest of all; cleanse our minds, we beseech Thee, by the inspiration of Thy Holy Spirit, that drawing near unto Thee with a pure heart and conscience undefiled, we may receive these Thy gifts without sin, and worthily magnify Thy holy name; through Jesus Christ our Lord. Amen." [14]

The growing tendency to dramatize the Sacrament by having the congregation and the minister partake of the bread and the wine at the same time is a reprehensible innovation, although the custom has the authority of the Moravian Liturgy. The Sacrament itself is the great drama.

The Sacrament should be celebrated with reverence and dignity, and this can best be done by following a ritual form, simple or elaborate as the minister and congregation may desire. In Episcopal Churches, which provide the worshipers with *The Book of Common Prayer*, the service can be followed by everyone, and this is greatly to be desired. It would be of great help to communicants if each one had the service in his hand which is used by the minister. The ritual used by all Methodist Churches is printed in the hymnal, and that is a custom to be commended. Sometimes one sees the Sacrament administered by an older minister who cares little for printed form. He has never had a book of forms. With the New Testament in his hand, or perhaps in his heart, he has celebrated the Holy Communion with dignity and grace, and the worshipers have felt the presence of the Unseen.

The celebration of the Sacrament, when properly administered, includes certain elements which are essential and which are present whether a prescribed order is followed or the service is conducted without a book of forms. What are these essentials that belong to the proper administration of the Sacrament? There must be the presence of the elements. " What kind of bread and wine are to be used, in what place or relative positions and postures the givers and receivers are to set themselves, and in what particular form and time the sacred actions are to be performed, are matters that cannot be certainly determined from Scripture; and are therefore to be decided by the light of nature and Christian prudence, according to the general principles laid down in the Word of God." [15]

In the second place, the Word of God is essential. There can be no Sacrament without the words of our Lord himself. The Sacrament enshrines the words of Christ and the words of the institution of the Supper must always have a place in the celebration. Christ is present in the Sacrament in his own words. They are his words. Luther, as well as Calvin, always emphasized the Word of God as part of the Sacrament. Luther again and again stated that it is not the water of baptism, nor the bread and the wine, that have efficacy, but the Word of God which accompanies the elements and our faith which relies on the Word of God. " The office of the sacraments," said Calvin, " is precisely the same as that of the word of God; which is to offer and present Christ to us, and in him the treasures of his heavenly grace." [16] The words of the institution of the Sacrament appear in every true celebration. Usually they are read as they appear in the eleventh chapter of First Corinthians. They are repeated when the elements are given to the people. In giving the bread, the minister says in effect, " The Lord Jesus took bread, and when He had blest it, He broke it, and gave it to His disciples, as I, ministering in His name, give this bread to you: saying, Take, eat; this is my body, broken for you: this do in remembrance of me." [17] In like manner, in administering the wine, after pouring the wine into the chalice on the table, he holds it up in the sight of the people, saying: "After the same manner our Saviour took the cup, and, having given thanks, as hath been done in His name, He gave it to His disciples; saying, This cup is the New Testament in my blood. Drink ye, all, of it." [18] The words are as essential as the elements, and even the Roman Church gives expression to this conviction. As part of the Communion ritual the priest says: "Who on the day before He suffered took bread into His holy and adorable hands, and lifting up His eyes to heaven, unto Thee, His Father, God Almighty, gave thanks to Thee, blessed, brake and gave it to His disciples, saying, Take and eat ye all of this, For this is My Body. Likewise after supper, taking also this most excellent chalice into His holy and adorable hands, and giving thanks to Thee, He blessed and gave it to His disciples, saying, Take and drink ye all of it, For this is the Cup of My Blood of the New and Everlasting Testament, the Mystery of Faith, which shall be shed for you and for many for the Remission of Sins. As oft as ye shall do this, ye shall do it in remembrance of Me." [19]

The third essential in the proper celebration of the Sacrament is the prayer that precedes the administration of the elements. It is the prayer of consecration, the prayer of thanksgiving, the Eucharistic prayer, known in Christian liturgy as the epiklesis, the prayer that invokes the blessing of the Holy Spirit upon the Sacrament, for without his blessing the ordinance is of no effect. No sacramental service is complete without some such invocation. It should be pointed out that the epiklesis, although possessing through the centuries a certain definite form, may not follow a historic pattern. The Lutheran and Moravian rituals, for example, have no such prayer, and in the services the words of the institution are considered the supreme act of consecration. The invocation of the Holy Spirit is not dependent upon any set form of words and may find expression in a hymn.

When the service is considered as a unity, care should be exercised regarding every detail. The minister himself should see that prayers, preaching, and music, both hymns and anthems, contribute to the meaning and message of the Sacrament. Here something may be said regarding the choice of music. It is worthy of consideration whether the same hymns and the same anthems may not be used at every Communion with increasing value. In this way they become part of the service itself, and as the years go by a certain significance becomes attached to them. They are kept sacred for the Communion service only and are not used at the regular services. Whether this is done or not, it is the primary duty of the minister to give particular attention to the choice of hymns. The first or opening hymn should be one of adoration and praise. It should sound the note of the greatness of God, his glory and his grace. It need not be a distinctive Communion hymn. It should be a hymn that is objective rather than subjective, and that centers the thought of the congregation upon the holiness of God. The following are hymns that may be used:

" Holy, Holy, Holy! Lord God Almighty! "
" Praise, My Soul, the King of Heaven."
" Our God, Our Help in Ages Past."
" O Worship the King All Glorious Above."
" O Thou My Soul, Bless God the Lord."
" The King of Love My Shepherd Is."
" The Church's One Foundation."
" I Love Thy Kingdom, Lord."
" God of Our Life, Through All the Circling Years."
" The Lord's My Shepherd, I'll Not Want."
" Crown Him with Many Crowns."
" Spirit of God, Descend Upon My Heart."

The second hymn is usually the Communion hymn. It should be one that points to Christ and to his sacrifice on the cross, and it should express not only contrition but gratitude. Too many of our Communion hymns are subjective and are frequently morbid. The Communion hymn should point to Christ, his sacrifice, and our identification with him in the act of Communion. In this connection the mood and temperament of the minister will probably determine the choice, but he will remember that the prayers are " common " prayers, and in like manner the praise also should be " common " praise. The hymns in our best hymnals selected for use in connection with the Sacrament are usually wisely chosen. The following may be suggested:

> " Jesus, to Thy Table Led."
> " Jesus, Thou Joy of Loving Hearts."
> " According to Thy Gracious Word."
> " When I Survey the Wondrous Cross."
> " Jesus, the Very Thought of Thee."
> " Bread of the World in Mercy Broken."
> " O Bread of Life from Heaven."
> " I Heard the Voice of Jesus Say."
> " Just as I Am, Without One Plea."
> " Thy Life Was Given for Me."
> " O My Saviour, Lifted."
> " There Is a Green Hill Far Away."

The singing of the hymn, " Break Thou the Bread of Life," should be avoided, since it refers, not to the Sacrament, but to the Scriptures.

The closing hymn requires careful consideration. It may be a Communion hymn, such as:

> " A Parting Hymn We Sing."
> " For the Bread, Which Thou Hast Broken."
> " Here, O My Lord, I See Thee Face to Face."

It may be a hymn of consecration, such as:

" O Jesus, I Have Promised."
" Saviour!   Thy Dying Love."
" O Master, Let Me Walk with Thee."
" O Jesus, Thou Art Standing."
" Love Divine, All Loves Excelling."
" Rock of Ages, Cleft for Me."
" Jesus, Lover of My Soul."
" Jesus, I Live to Thee."

It may be a hymn of exultation and thanksgiving, the service thus closing upon a triumphant note.   The following hymns are suggested:

" Jesus Shall Reign Where'er the Sun."
" The Head That Once Was Crowned with Thorns."
" When All Thy Mercies, O My God."
" All Hail the Power of Jesus' Name! "
" O for a Thousand Tongues to Sing."
" Rise, My Soul, and Stretch Thy Wings."
" Lead On, O King Eternal."

The hymn, " For All the Saints Who from Their Labors Rest," has much to commend it.   It is in keeping with the closing Communion prayer, which should be a prayer of commemoration of the departed.   If this hymn is sung at the close of each Communion, a definite impression concerning the Church Invisible, the communion of saints on earth and in heaven, is created and comfort and strength given to those who at Communion seasons feel intensely the loss of loved ones.

If anthems are used in the Communion service, the minister should, in consultation with the director of the music, make the selection.   This part of the service should not be neglected or ignored.   It is of vital importance.   The whole Sacrament may be robbed of its spiritual value by the introduction of music that has no relation to the sacred rite.   Better far to have none than to introduce something that harms rather than helps.   The anthems should be short and sacramental in both words and music.   The following contain the true note and may be helpful to ministers seeking guidance in a realm in which they may not have competent knowledge:

Composer	Title	Publisher
Bortniansky	" Divine Praise "	Oliver Ditson Company, Inc.
Christiansen	" O Bread of Life "	Augsburg Publishing House
Candlyn	" Thee We Adore "	Carl Fischer, Inc.
Dickinson	" Beneath the Shadow "	The H. W. Gray Company, Inc.
Elgar	" Jesus, Word of God Incarnate "	Novello & Co., Ltd.
Franck	" O Bread of Life from Heaven "	Oliver Ditson Company, Inc.
Gale	" Come Unto Me "	The John Church Company
Gounod	" Sanctus "	G. Schirmer, Inc.
Holst	" Let All Mortal Flesh "	G. Schirmer, Inc.
Moore	" O Saviour of the World "	Novello & Co., Ltd.
Mozart	" Jesus, Word of God Incarnate "	Novello & Co., Ltd.
Palestrina	" O Saviour of the World "	Novello & Co., Ltd.
Rachmaninoff	" Glory to the Trinity "	J. Fischer & Bro.
Whitlock	" Here, O My Lord, I See Thee Face to Face "	Oxford University Press
Wichmann	" O Lamb of God "	Volkwein
Willan	" Very Bread, Good Shepherd Tend Us "	The H. W. Gray Company, Inc.

In the service of the Holy Communion, limitation rather than change and variety should guide our selection of hymns and anthems. By the repetition of the same music at each Communion they become part of the ritual, and an atmosphere of priceless value is created.

The question as to how frequently the Sacrament should be observed raises questions difficult to answer. Certain it is that historically the Early Church observed it every Sunday, and that practice was continued until the Reformation. Calvin and Bucer wished to continue the weekly observances. Knox apparently was satisfied with a monthly observance. In Scotland in the sixteenth century it was observed in the country twice, and in towns four times, a year. Later it was celebrated once a year, and during the period of the Commonwealth it was often neglected altogether. It would seem that, since the Sacrament is central in Christian worship and has the same function as the Word, it ought to be more frequently celebrated than is done in many Churches.

Another question of importance relates to the conduct of the service while the congregation receives the elements. The congregation may be large and much time needed for the distribution. Sometimes familiar hymns are played on the organ or the minister reads portions of appropriate Scripture or a hymn is sung. The purpose is to guide the meditation of the people. There is, however, a growing tendency to maintain silence. In these days when people are seldom alone, this period of silence is a means of grace. It has the value of spiritual discipline. Perhaps at the preparatory service guidance can be given for the use of such a period of silence, and provision may be made for it. " Rightly used, the silence of a great congregation whilst communicating may be one of the most uplifting and inspiring influences that flow from the observance of the Sacrament. It has the inestimable advantage of providing a time when the voice of man being hushed, Christ is left free to speak His own word to the soul that waits upon Him." [20]

Since the entire service is a unity, care should be taken by the minister to understand the significance of each act and the reason for the various movements within the appointed order of celebration. It is unnecessary here to set down in detail the historic order. This can be found in any good book which provides forms and orders for the celebration of the sacraments in the Protestant communions. Every minister should have in his library a collection of these books. A few may here be mentioned:

The Book of Common Worship of the Presbyterian Church
    in the U.S.A.
The Book of Common Order of the Church of Scotland.
The Book of Common Prayer of the Protestant Episcopal
    Church.
The Book of Common Order of the United Church of Canada.
The Service Book and Ordinal of the Presbyterian Church of
    South Africa.

The Methodist Hymnal, containing the orders for the administration of the sacraments.
The Common Service Book of the United Lutheran Church in America.
The Liturgy of the Moravian Church.

The study of the forms and orders provided in these books will enrich the mind and sanctify the heart. They reveal the priceless treasure which the Church of Christ possesses and which should not be neglected.

The minister who carefully studies these rituals will discover the fact that what is called the Eucharistic prayer has much that is common to all the services. It contains the great thanksgiving, which has been offered in various forms since apostolic times. The prayer has remained substantially the same throughout the centuries. It ought to remain unchanged, and ministers render a disservice to their people when they seek to alter or " improve " upon it. The prayer begins with the salutation, " The Lord be with you," and the answering response, " And with thy spirit." It passes to the *sursum corda,* coming to us from the third century, " Lift up your hearts," and again the response, " We lift them up unto the Lord." Then the thanksgiving note is heard, " Let us give thanks unto our Lord God," and again the response, " It is meet and right so to do." Immediately the thanksgiving note is proclaimed: " It is very meet, right, and our bounden duty, that we should at all times, and in all places, give thanks unto Thee, O Lord, Holy Father, Almighty, Everlasting God; who didst create the heavens and the earth and all that in them is; who didst make man in Thine own image and whose tender mercies are over all Thy works." Then follows the response, from all created beings in earth and in heaven:

> " Holy, holy, holy, Lord God of Hosts,
> Heaven and earth are full of Thy glory:
> Glory be to Thee, O Lord Most High."

There is necessarily a period of silence before the prayer in which the redemptive work of Christ is commemorated continues. This prayer rehearses the sacrifice of Christ upon the cross — the full and perfect and sufficient sacrifice which he made for the sin of the whole world. His Incarnation, his holy life, his Passion, his death, Resurrection, and Ascension are remembered in gratitude and praise. These facts of the life and death of our Lord have always been retold in the Eucharistic prayer. Then follows the invocation for the Holy Spirit, known as the epiklesis, asking that the Holy Spirit may bless and sanctify " these Thine own gifts of Bread and Wine which we set before Thee, that we may receive by faith Christ crucified for us." Thus it is proclaimed that the Sacrament becomes effectual because of what God does, and not because of anything we do. The interpretation of the efficacy of this prayer divides Christendom. The Roman and Greek Catholic Churches hold that " after the consecration there is present under the appearances of bread not only Christ's Body, nor under the appearances of wine only His Blood, but under the appearances of either, and in every single portion of them, the whole and entire Jesus Christ, God and man." [21] The Westminster divines, speaking for the Protestant Reformation, in the Directory for Worship state the nature of the consecrating prayer: " Let the prayer, thanksgiving, or blessing of the bread and wine, be to this effect: Earnestly to pray to God, the Father of all mercies, and God of all consolation, to vouchsafe his gracious presence, and the effectual working of his Spirit in us; and so to sanctify these elements both of bread and wine, and to bless his own ordinance, that we may receive by faith the body and blood of Jesus Christ, crucified for us, and so to feed upon him, that he may be one with us, and we one with him; that he may live in us, and we in him, and to him who hath loved us, and given himself for us." [22]

This statement goes as far as interpretation can go, for the blessing of the Holy Spirit does not pertain to the details of the ordinance but to the ordinance itself. It is related to the sacramental act in its unity and includes everything — the elements, the words of institution, the symbolism of breaking the bread and pouring the wine, the administration, the faith of the believer. It is one Sacrament, one sacramental act, one sanctifying, symbolizing, and sealing act by the Holy Spirit. It is something God does for us.

The Eucharistic prayer closes with an offertory dedication in which, in response to Christ's gift of himself to us, we give ourselves to him: " And here we offer and present unto Thee ourselves, our souls and bodies, to be a reasonable, holy and living sacrifice unto Thee: praying that all we, who are partakers of this Holy Communion, may find that in this place Thou givest peace; through Jesus Christ our Lord; to whom with Thee and the Holy Spirit, be the glory and the praise, both now and evermore. Amen." [23] In the presence of such an act of consecration it is crucial that nothing be said or sung that would draw the mind of the worshiper away from what God is doing for him in and through the Sacrament. It is essentially a time when the prayer of our hearts may well be, " Speak, Lord; for thy servant heareth."

IX. Special Communion Services

SOMETIMES a false issue is raised between what is called " the pulpit and the altar." No such issue should arise. A true evangelical sermon presents Jesus Christ. So do the sacraments. They are the sacraments of the Gospel. Augustine called a sacrament a *verbum visibile,* " the Gospel made visible." Preaching requires a pulpit and a congregation, and when the congregation is large, preaching takes on new power. In the administration of the sacraments, however, the act is the same whether it takes place where two or three are gathered together in His name or in a vast cathedral before a hushed and uncounted congregation. The Sacrament was first observed in the upper room, and the early Christians continued to observe it from house to house. It is this adaptability to meet the needs of the many or of the few that makes possible frequency of Communion and the observance of special sacramental services.

Whether the Lord's Supper is observed weekly or monthly or quarterly, there are special occasions when it may be celebrated with great profit. It is the purpose of this chapter to suggest times and seasons when the Sacrament may be administered other than at the regular stated services of the Church. Whenever circumstances permit, it is wise to have the Sacrament celebrated in the sanctuary, where memories and sacred associations combine to minister to the spiritual life. Protestants do not make use of the Church so much as they should, and people need to be taught that the Church, as such, has something to contribute which cannot be received elsewhere. Sometimes a second Communion is celebrated on the same Sunday on which the regular service is held. There are many who cannot attend the Sunday-morning service at a special hour on a particular day, and they should not be deprived of receiving the Holy Communion. Justin Martyr suggests that after the weekly observance of the Sacrament, absent Christians were remembered and the Sacrament was taken to them. In that day there were slaves who were not masters of their own time. Today there are multitudes of men and women who do not command their own time. There are servants in homes, men and women on night shifts, chauffeurs and workmen, doctors and nurses, who labor while others rest but who desire the strength and comfort which the Sacrament affords. Services planned for such, in small or larger groups, are appreciated. Such a service may follow the order of the morning Communion, or if there be a small group who desire to communicate, it may be held immediately following the evening service or, under specially appointed conditions, in the chapel. There are many who desire the greater intimacy provided by a chapel service. In many service books a short order for the celebration of the Communion is provided, but the minister will know best what to do.

There are high occasions in the Church year when the celebration of the Sacrament is most appropriate. The observance of the Church year, which is becoming more prevalent, brings the great events of the Christian faith to attention. From Advent and Christmas we move on to Lent and Easter, to Ascension Day and Whitsunday. The great festivals — Christmas, Easter, Pentecost — furnish exceptional opportunities for the observance of Holy Communion. Such days are sacred through long Christian usage. It is becoming more and more customary to celebrate the Sacrament on Thursday evening of Holy Week, the same night on which the Supper was instituted.

There are also occasions when the Sacrament may be administered in the sanctuary to one person, or two, or to a family or a group. Young ministers, especially, should think through the possibilities latent in such opportunities and begin early to make provision for them. There certainly needs to be a new emphasis placed upon marriage. It is customary for young people to come to the minister, in his home or in his study, to make arrangements for the wedding ceremony. They come with all their finest instincts of spiritual aspiration stirring within them. They stand together on the threshold of a new life and a new world. Instead of treating their loving relation lightly, giving expression to some word of pleasantry, ignoring the solemn vows which they are about to take, the minister can use the occasion for the highest purposes. Perhaps one of them is not a Christian, or they may be members of different Churches. They may need instruction and guidance as to what marriage means, for while we do not hold that marriage is a sacrament, we believe that it is a solemn and sacred ordinance instituted by God and that it is the most sacred relationship in life. Charles Kingsley once said, " The highest state I define as that state through and in which man can know most of God, and work most for God: and this I assert to be the marriage state." [1] What could be more fitting than that these young people should be invited to partake of the Sacrament at some appointed hour before their marriage? They would feel, thereby, an added sacredness attached to the new relationship upon which they were entering and a new devotion to Christ and his Church.

There are many occasions when a quiet Communion service may be held in the church or in the chapel. There are times of sorrow when fathers and mothers are deeply concerned about themselves and their children. Someone whom they love better than life has brought shame and disgrace; perhaps death has entered the home and left a man or a woman desolate; or a boy or girl has come home from college with a new interest in the Christian life and is ready to be received into communicant membership in the Church. Here, for example, is a young man who has been inducted into the Army or the Navy. In a few days he will be leaving home, and his family may not see him again for months or years, or perhaps never. There is anxiety and solicitude for him on the part of his parents. They all seek strength and courage for the unknown future. They are invited to come to the sanctuary at a definite hour and there partake together of the Holy Communion. It is an occasion for deep and lasting value and, in the strength of it, they go forward to their varied tasks. All such occasions are opportunities for pastoral service, and by the administration of the Sacrament the seal of God is given to purposes and decisions. Every minister knows the futility of much of what is called parish visitation. Often it is a waste of time and accomplishes little or nothing; often it serves only to arrest criticism and to satisfy the clerical conscience. Yet here is one situation where the pastoral function may be enriched and magnified.

There are circumstances, however, when people cannot come to the sanctuary. Such occasions happen in homes and hospitals. They concern probably only one person, or the immediate members of the family. In every congregation there are elderly persons who cannot attend Church services. All their lives they have been faithful communicants. The sacramental Sunday has been a marked day in their thoughts, and when the Sacrament is celebrated for them in their homes their loyalty to the Church is maintained and their devotion to Christ deepened. There are also members of the Church who have been sick for prolonged periods and have been deprived of the comfort and strength of the services of the Church. Communion seasons go by and they follow what goes on in the Church with prayerful solicitude. It may be that the illness is sudden and serious, and there is an expressed desire for the help the Holy Communion brings. The minister must be careful not to thrust the Sacrament upon those who are fearful and who may associate it with what the Roman Church calls the last rites or extreme unction. There are men and women who shrink from emotional crises. They react unfavorably even when prayer is offered. To a minister who came in the night at the doctor's request to pray with a very sick woman, the greeting was, " Am I as bad as that? " She thought the minister had been called because the doctor had failed. Nowhere is spiritual sensitiveness needed more than in the sickroom, and nowhere is it more appreciated. Careful inquiry on the part of the minister through the family or a friend will save him from hurting where he would like to help.

In preparing to celebrate the Sacrament in the home or hospital great care should be taken to follow the proper sacramental order. Unless the situation calls for immediate silence and promptness, the minister is expected not to hurry but to tarry and visit in a normal and natural manner. It may be that the person is an old friend and that age has hindered him from attending the Church service, or perhaps the sick person is convalescing and gratitude is outspoken. There is no reason why visitation may not be helpful, but when the time arrives for the observance of the Sacrament, it alone should be allowed to speak. The table should be prepared and the elements made ready with order and dignity. The minister, if it is his custom, may wear his gown. The order for the service, though brief, should contain all the elements essential to the Sacrament, and when the celebration is concluded the minister should depart, allowing the ordinance to give its own message. Conversation of a general character after the celebration should be avoided. The closing prayer should do all that is necessary by way of intimate or personal intercession.

In recent years a great advance has been made by the appointment of hospital chaplains, and the association which these chaplains have organized has given to the hospital a much-needed religious service. Through the chaplain provision is made for the celebration of the Communion for the staff, for the nurses, and for such patients as can come to the chapel or hall. Frequently the Communion is held in the hospital at the time of the great festivals of the Church: Christmas, Easter, Pentecost. It has become possible in some institutions to have a public address system installed, so that patients in private rooms may follow the service and, at their request, be served the Communion in their rooms. In this way sacred traditions are established in hospitals, sanitariums, homes, and prisons, and such services are anticipated by those who are responsible for the welfare of the institutions. In almost every parish such opportunities are open to those who have eyes to see and hands to serve.

The growing influence of summer camps and conferences for young people is one of the encouraging signs of our day. Thousands of young men and women in all parts of our country, and in other countries, gather for Bible study and discussion concerning the Christian way of life, and it is fitting and natural at the close, after there has been searching of heart and life decisions, that there should be a desire to partake together of the Holy Communion. Sometimes the Sacrament can be observed in a lovely chapel; again it may be celebrated in a barnlike structure, or in the open air. Those in charge should be careful to see that the Sacrament is observed with reverence, dignity, and order. There should be no attempt to alter the service, to experiment with it, or to put it in the hands of those who have not been duly appointed by the Church to perform such service. Furthermore, attention should be paid to the restrictions under which certain young people worship. They should not be asked to violate their Church vows, for there are Churches which do not approve of inter-Communion, and this fact should be recognized. In the administration of the Sacrament, therefore, care should be taken that it be done under the supervision of those who are set apart or approved by the Church for such service.

These are days when many young men and women have been uprooted from their homes and Churches and are crowded in new industrial areas and in war camps in the homeland and abroad. In these areas unusual obligation rests upon chaplains and Churches. There is increasing evidence that no worship service meets the need of men in war areas, in camps, in the front line, on ships, as does the Holy Communion, and the reports that come emphasize this fact. Here is a letter from a British chaplain serving in North Africa. It is typical and is given for its encouragement concerning the efficacy of the

Sacrament in its unifying and uplifting power, and for the hope it inspires. The chaplain writes: " I had a really fine Easter Day, having eight Communion services in the morning, and a parade service covering a large area. During one of the Communion services for the English troops at a war prisoners' camp, I noticed a crowd of about forty to fifty Germans standing in a group, very quietly and reverently, watching the service go on. After the service I asked the British officer in charge whether there were any German Protestants among the prisoners. He said he would find out and phone me up at lunch time. He did so, and astounded me by telling me that eighty of them were asking for Communion. I then arranged to hold a service for them at three o'clock that afternoon (Easter Sunday). The authorities allowed me to go into the camp where the Germans lived, alone, without any guard or other Englishman present. There I found a large tent full of Germans waiting for me (about 120 to 130 of them), and a tall, good-looking German N.C.O., who spoke English perfectly, to act as interpreter. I got him to explain what the service was. He replied, ' They know it, sir.' So I took the service, in English of course, getting this N.C.O. to explain in various parts of the service what the particular prayer was about. I got him to preface the prayer for the Church militant with prayers for the brotherhood of man amongst all nations with Christ as our Leader. I had a white Communion cloth on the table, with cross (a large one), and candlesticks (lighted candles). The Germans themselves had placed the table for me with a clean blanket to cover it. When I asked the German N.C.O. to get those to put up their hands who wanted to receive Communion, almost the whole lot put up their hands. They came in twelves, and knelt to receive in a most orderly and reverent manner. None would touch the chalice, but all just raised their chins a little. One hundred and nine received Communion. Then I told the N.C.O. that I was about to continue the service with the Lord's Prayer, saying that if they wished to say it themselves then they could follow me as I said it in

English. Everyone immediately stood to attention and, in very loud deep voices, recited our Lord's Prayer. It was a moving experience. I finished the service with the blessing, and then told the German N.C.O. that as a Christian brother I would like to shake them by the hand, if they so wished. They all filed by me, stood stiffly to attention, bowed, shook hands, and tried to say thank you. Some could speak English, and thanked me very much for giving them that service. One German told me that he was a Christian missionary before the war, and was most grateful on his own behalf, and on behalf of his fellow Germans, for having the opportunity of making their Easter Communion. He spoke English perfectly. This morning I went up to the camp and gave him a New Testament and a small service prayer book. He said it was just what he wanted, not only for himself, but so that he could have services amongst his friends. They all moved from here this afternoon." This is a testimony for which we are profoundly grateful and one that constitutes a challenge to the Christian Church.

The very fact that such occasions furnish exceptional opportunities demands, on the part of all ministers, sensitiveness to the needs of their people and their community. Frequently great national crises arise. A war begins. A war suddenly ends. Some overwhelming tragedy casts a shadow over life. It may be a flood, a mine disaster, a railroad wreck, and silence takes possession of families and of the entire community. In such circumstances, the Roman Catholic Church celebrates Mass and offers prayers for the repose of the souls of the dead. What is expected of the Protestant Church? Has it something to say, something to give? Certainly it has, but too frequently the Church doors are closed.

No rule can be laid down, but a principle can be established. Nothing should be done to detract from the regular Communion service. It is there, in fellowship with the people of God, that the needs of congregations are met, but that will not interfere with the observance of the Sacrament at times and occasions when there is special need on the part of individuals, families, and groups. The sacrament of the Lord's Supper is indeed a Communion service, a fellowship with Christ and with Christ's Church. It is also a " sealing " of Christ and his salvation to the individual believer, and that act may be one of sanctified solitude when the Saviour says, " Come unto me," and the response is made, " O Lamb of God, I come! "

X. The Service Preparatory to the Communion

THE word "preparation" has sacred associations. Mark speaks of "the Preparation, that is, the day before the sabbath." To the Jews, the Sabbath was a day of feasting, but the food was prepared on the preceding day, the day of preparation. The early Christians took over the word, and even today it is the regular word for Friday in the Greek calendar. It is used in this sense in the *Didache*, but later the name was applied also to the day preceding any sacred festival. Whether or not the use of the name has any relation to what we call "The Service Preparatory to the Communion" is doubtful, but the same idea which inspired one would also initiate the other. It is natural that preparation should precede holy days and holy fasts and festivals, and, above all, sacramental occasions. The Westminster Directory for Worship instructs the minister that "it is requisite that publick warning be given the sabbath-day before the administration thereof: and that either then, or on some day of that week, something concerning that ordinance, and the due preparation thereunto, and participation thereof, be taught; that, by the diligent use of all means sanctified of God to that end, both in publick and private, all may come better prepared to that heavenly feast." [1] There is here all the guidance needed for personal and public preparation.

It has, of course, always been recognized that some form of personal preparation is necessary before partaking of the Holy Communion. This has been the practice since the earliest times. Justin Martyr states that catechumens were accustomed to fast before baptism and that the whole Church fasted with them. Tertullian tells us that before partaking of the Eucharist communicants prepared themselves by fasting. The Roman Church sets down definite and precise rules that should be observed by those preparing to partake of the Holy Communion. The communicant is required " to distinguish table from table, this sacred table from profane tables, this celestial bread from common bread. This we do when we firmly believe, that the Eucharist really and truly contains the body and the blood of the Lord." Secondly, " we should . . . carefully examine our consciences, lest perhaps they be defiled by mortal guilt, which sincere repentance alone can efface." Thirdly, " we should also reflect in the silence of our own hearts, how unworthy we are that God should bestow on us this divine gift." Fourthly, " we should also put the question to ourselves, whether we can truly say with Peter: ' Lord, thou knowest that I love thee.' " Fifthly, " our preparation should not, however, be confined to the soul: it should also extend to the body. We are to approach the Holy Eucharist fasting, having neither eaten nor drunk, at least from the preceding midnight." [2] The Roman Church further decrees " that none may be deterred by the difficulty of the preparation from approaching the Holy Eucharist, the faithful are frequently to be reminded that they are all bound to receive this sacrament; and that the Church has decreed that whoever neglects to approach the Holy Communion once a year, at Easter, subjects himself to sentence of excommunication." [3]

It is set forth in the New Testament that faithful preparation should precede the sacramental fellowship of the faithful. Paul placed great emphasis upon the necessity of self-examination. Long before the custom grew up in Scotland of " fencing the tables " he warned the Church of Corinth against secularizing the Sacrament. " Whosoever," he says, " shall eat the bread or drink the cup of the Lord in an unworthy manner, shall be guilty of the body and the blood of the Lord. But let a man prove himself, and so let him eat of the bread, and drink of the cup. For he that eateth and drinketh, eateth and drinketh judgment unto himself, if he discern not the body." [4]

The people of Corinth were eating and drinking " unworthily " and thus bringing judgment upon themselves. Personal self-examination is necessary on the part of all those who would receive help from the Holy Communion. Such self-interrogation is not for the purpose of creating a morbid attitude toward this sacred ordinance, but in order that, by means of meditation and reflection upon the sacrifice of Christ, we may be able to " discern " the Lord's body. Each of us will be able to formulate our own order of examination preparatory to the Lord's Supper. A distinguished layman told his pastor that he never went to the Communion service without first reading the story of our Lord's Passion and death. Truly that is a good habit. Those who come to the Sacrament are to examine themselves on " being in Christ; of their sins and wants; of the truth and measures of their knowledge, faith, repentance, love to God and the brethren, charity to all men, forgiving those that have done them wrong; of their desires after Christ; and of their new obedience: and by renewing the exercise of these graces, by serious meditation, and fervent prayer." [5] Each communicant will discover for himself the best method by which he may prepare himself. It may be by reading passages from the Gospels or the Epistles. It may be by using a guide to meditation and prayer. It may be by reading through the hymns appointed for use in connection with the sacramental service. It may be through silence and the observance of a quiet hour. Help may be found in the many fine books of personal devotion that are available and among these one of the best is *Of the Imitation of Christ,* by Thomas à Kempis. In this immortal book there is a long last section entitled " Concerning the Communion." It contains a heart-searching examination of personal conduct and character with confession of unworthiness. " Alas," he says, " how little is that which I do! how short a time do I spend when I am preparing myself to receive the communion! Seldom am I wholly collected; very seldom indeed am I cleansed from all distraction. And yet surely in the life-giving presence of thy Godhead no unbecoming thought ought to intrude itself, nor should any creature occupy my heart; for it is not an angel, but the Lord of angels, whom I am about to entertain. . . . Why therefore am I not more ardent and zealous in seeking thine adorable presence? . . . Thanks be unto thee, O merciful Jesu, thou eternal shepherd, that thou hast vouchsafed to refresh us, who are poor and in a state of banishment, with thy precious body and blood, and to invite us to the receiving of these mysteries with the words even of thine own mouth, saying, ' Come unto me all ye that labour and are heavy laden and I will refresh you.' " [6]

Preparation for the observance of the Lord's Supper pertains, however, not only to persons but also to congregations. The Directory for Worship, as authorized by the Presbyterian Church, makes reference to this custom in these words: " As it has been customary, in some parts of our Church, to observe a fast before the Lord's Supper; to have a sermon on Saturday and Monday; and to invite two or three ministers on such occasions; and as these seasons have been blessed to many souls, and may tend to keep up a stricter union of ministers and congregations; we think it not improper that they who choose it may continue in this practice." [7] The Westminster divines were not eager to see continued in the Reformed Churches such oecasions as Lent, Good Friday, Easter, Christmas, Pentecost, for such were for them associated with Rome. They were not opposed, however, to the observance of fasts when occasions demanded, and while holy days, except Sunday, were discountenanced, pre-Communion and post-Communion services became customary in Scotland and in Colonial America. The post-Communion service on Thanksgiving Monday dates back to 1630 following a remarkable revival, the result of the preaching of John Livingstone. The origin of the Thursday fast, and the Friday and Saturday services, is obscure, and information must be found in diaries and sessional and presbyterial records. In his illuminating study of the Presbyterians in America, William Warren Sweet sums up the results of his

investigations in these words: "The administration of the
Lord's Supper on the Sabbath was, however, but the culmina-
tion of a series of meetings which generally began on Thursday, which was observed as a day of fasting and prayer. There
were usually services also on Saturday and the Monday following. The families residing in the vicinity of the meeting
were usually thronged with lodgers, and people came from
relatively long distances and remained for several days together, which gave them an opportunity for pleasant social
intercourse, and the young people a chance to become ac-
quainted. Indeed we are told that such meetings paved the
way for many a happy marriage." 8

In the remarkable story *Old Redstone*, which has become a
veritable source book, we find similar information. There we
read that " the communion seasons for our fathers were, from
an early period, exceedingly interesting. The Thursday preceding was commonly observed as a day of fasting and prayer.
And there was always public worship on Saturday and Monday, in connexion with these occasions. The ministers, of
course, aided each other; and many people from surrounding
congregations and distant settlements attended. The families residing in the vicinity of the place were usually thronged
with lodgers. Though there was much, in all the circumstances of these meetings, calculated to produce a species of
religious dissipation, we cannot but believe they were eminently profitable and refreshing seasons, and greatly aided in
extending the influence of the gospel through those early settlements. The extension of the services through several successive days contributed to suspend or lighten the influence
of their worldly cares, and to break up, for a time, their
anxieties and all their little petty vexations of domestic life.
They promoted, also, Christian fellowship, and enlarged the
sphere of their social intercourse and of their Christian sym-
pathies. They paved the way for many happy marriages and
many auspicious nuptials. Above all, they proved seasons of
special intercourse with heaven, and of foretaste of its joys,

to many of those greatly tried and often sorrowing Christians who, in their frontier life, were frequently in heaviness through manifold temptations. It is worthy of special notice, also, that a very large proportion of those who were brought from darkness to light, and from the power of Satan unto God — traced their first religious impressions to these sacramental seasons." [9]

This custom of holding preparatory services belongs especially to the Presbyterian tradition, and in the United States, Canada, Australia, South Africa, and especially in Scotland, such services are still strongly supported and productive of great good. There are still Churches that maintain a Saturday-afternoon service with good results. It is probable, however, that this good custom is declining, and such a tendency is to be regretted. It has been found difficult to maintain the weekly prayer meeting, and it occasions no surprise that the preparatory service suffers from the same pressure of modern life, the increasing prestige of amusement, the unsettled conditions due to the war, and to the multiplication of meetings and services in the Church itself. Furthermore, the increased frequency of the celebration of the Communion has made it less exceptional in the life of the Church than when it was celebrated only once a year. It was then the one annual event of surpassing importance in the life of the community, and it was not only a religious but a social occasion of exceptional importance.

There is probably, however, another reason for the decline of the service. The minister may be to blame for obscuring the importance of the preparatory service, and for not preparing adequately for it. Too frequently it has become just another devotional service, without definite purpose or sacramental reference, and the people have taken less and less interest in it. Its central purpose has not been recognized, and if renewed interest is desired, then the Church as well as the minister should face the question, What do we seek to accomplish in having such a service? The Church of Scotland answers the question by placing in its *Book of Common Order* a complete order for the preparatory service. It contains not only an order of worship but complete prayers, so beautifully and appropriately worded that in themselves they constitute an uplifting experience. It has been the custom in many communities, and is so still, that the preparatory service has certain obligations of its own. Instead of new members' being received at the Sunday celebration of the Communion, they are received at the preparatory service, when occasion is given for Christian fellowship and congregational and personal friendship. There is much to commend in this custom, and it could be introduced with profit to those who are uniting with the Church and to the congregation itself. Furthermore, in days when " tokens " were used, and so-called " close " Communion followed, it was at the preparatory service that distribution was made and all arrangements ordered, so that nothing needed to be done or said when the Holy Communion was celebrated. It is easily understood, therefore, that the preparatory service had a definite place in the life and work of the Church, and if it is to re-establish itself it must regain a place and value of its own. It should, of course, minister to the need of today. The minister and the Church officers should set themselves seriously to think how this service may best strengthen the spiritual life of the Church.

There is the *setting*. Why should not the service be held in the Church sanctuary with choir present and with everything pertaining to Church worship at its best? The missionary motto applies here: " Expect great things from God. Attempt great things for God." The words of our Lord take on new meaning in this connection. " He sendeth two of his disciples, and saith unto them, Go into the city, and there shall meet you a man bearing a pitcher of water: follow him; and wheresoever he shall enter in, say to the master of the house, The Teacher saith, Where is my guest-chamber, where I shall eat the passover with my disciples? And he will himself show you a large upper room furnished and ready:

and there make ready for us." [10]   One would like to see that
" large upper room furnished and ready," which still was not
quite ready, but which was made ready at the command of the
Lord.   When little is expected, little is achieved.   When communicant members are allowed to treat this important service
lightly, the result is disquieting.

There is the *music*.   The hymns and anthems should have
the same care in their selection as in the Communion service
itself.   They should be familiar, and one or two may be repeated at each preparatory service so that a helpful association may be developed.   The music should center upon the
purpose of the service, but should not be the same as is used
at the Sunday Communion.   A few hymns may be suggested:

> " O Jesus, Thou Art Standing."
> " O Love That Wilt Not Let Me Go."
> " I Heard the Voice of Jesus Say."
> " Saviour! Thy Dying Love."
> " Jesus, the Very Thought of Thee."
> " Just as I Am, Without One Plea."
> " Thy Life Was Given for Me."
> " Art Thou Weary, Heavy-laden."
> " Rock of Ages, Cleft for Me."
> " Jesus, Lover of My Soul."
> " Beneath the Cross of Jesus."
> " Cross of Jesus, Cross of Sorrow."
> " There Is a Green Hill Far Away."
> " Lord Jesus, When We Stand Afar."
> " O My Saviour, Lifted."

These same hymns should be used also in the Church School,
so that children and young people may become familiar with
them and in this way be prepared for communicant Church
membership.   In like manner, when solo or anthem music is
used, oversight should be exercised by the minister to the end
that the whole service will be a unity, concentrating upon
the main purpose.

There are the *prayers*. The minister may prepare himself in his own way for this important service, or he may make use of forms of prayers which have been consecrated by long usage in the Christian Church. If such prayers are used regularly at this service, they become familiar and in time rich in association. A complete order with appropriate prayers, may be found in *The Book of Common Order* of the Church of Scotland, and in the new edition of *The Book of Common Worship* of the Presbyterian Church in the U. S. A. With such suggestions in his possession, the minister can prepare his own service. It may be built around the Beatitudes. After each Beatitude there may be a period of silence followed by a brief petition expressing the thought of the Beatitude. It may be built around the Commandments, following the same suggestive order. A beautiful service may be arranged by reading the story of the Passion and cross of Christ, as given in a harmony of the Gospels, with suitable hymns such as have been already suggested. This prayer, with a few minor changes, used in the Moravian Liturgy gives the needed approach:

> Lord God, Father in Heaven,
> > *Have mercy upon us.*
> Lord God, Son, Thou Saviour of the world,
> > *Be gracious unto us.*
> Lord God, Holy Ghost,
> > *Abide with us forever.*
> From all sin,
> From all error,
> From all evil,
> > *Preserve us, gracious Lord and God.*
> From pestilence and famine,
> From calamity by fire or water, hail or tempest,
> From war and bloodshed,
> From the violence of wicked men,
> > *Preserve us, gracious Lord and God.*
> From indifference to Thy merits and death,
> From pride and self-complacency,

From needless perplexity,
From the unhappy desire of becoming great,
From hypocrisy and fanaticism,
From envy, hatred, and malice,
From the deceitfulness of sin,
From the influence of the spirit of this world,
     Preserve us, gracious Lord and God.
By all the merits of Thy life,
By Thy human birth,
By Thy obedience, diligence, and faithfulness,
By Thy humility, meekness, and patience,
By Thy extreme poverty,
By Thy baptism, fasting, and temptation,
By Thy griefs and sorrows,
By Thy prayers and tears,
By Thy having been despised and rejected,
     Bless and comfort us, gracious Lord and God.
By Thy agony and bloody sweat,
By Thy bonds and scourging,
By Thy crown of thorns,
By Thy cross and passion,
By Thy dying words,
By Thy atoning death,
By Thy glorious resurrection and ascension,
By Thy sitting at the right hand of God,
By Thy sending the Holy Spirit,
By Thy prevailing intercession,
By Thy holy sacraments,
By Thy divine presence,
By Thy coming again to Thy Church on earth,
  or our being called home to Thee,
     Bless and comfort us, gracious Lord and God.

There is the *preaching.* The sermon should have a direct bearing upon the Sacrament itself. General themes, even though they be based on some passage of Scripture, are often out of place. There may be wide variety of choice and yet the sermon may move within the true sacramental orbit. The theme of the cross is always fitting and is expected by devout Christians. A distinguished judge said to his minister, "I come to the preparatory service because I formed the habit as a young man, but I am disappointed when I am not brought face to face with the fact of sin and the mercy of the cross." There is a wealth of material in the story of the Passion of Christ, and a young minister would do well both for himself and his people if he would construct his program of preparatory sermons around these crucial passages. Scholars have found in the account of the Passion, as recorded in Matthew, Mark, and Luke, that the events follow the same order, and it is highly probable that the Passion narrative itself was part of the kerygma of the Early Church. They find in each of the Gospels nine episodes: the observance of the Last Supper, the prophecy of the treachery of Judas, the betrayal and arrest in the Garden, the trial before the high priest, the trial before Pilate, the Crucifixion, the burial, the empty tomb, the Resurrection appearances. What better method could a minister adopt than this which is implicit in the Passion narratives? There are, also, the personalities assembled around the cross: Judas, Pilate, Herod, Caiaphas, the two thieves, the centurion, the disciples. There are the seven words spoken by Jesus from the cross. There is our Lord's own attitude toward the cross, his anticipation of it, and his acceptance of it. This is the sermon theme. "The supreme subject of doctrinal preaching," says Henry Sloane Coffin, " is the Cross of Christ. One has only to measure the relative space given it in the New Testament, not only in the epistles but in all four gospels, to gain an idea of the proportionate attention it should receive in the teaching of those who wish to be guided by the New Testament balance." [11] There is rich and neglected sermon material in the doctrine of the Sacrament itself. Many ministers seem to be utterly unmindful of the possibilities which are available in this area, and yet they wonder why laymen do not possess the same Church consciousness that belongs to men who were trained under ministers conscious of the need for instruction concerning the sacraments. There is material here for many years of good preaching, and it would be welcomed by intelligent Church members. Here are some of the questions to which the sermon may be the response: What is a sacrament? How do the sacraments become effectual means to salvation? What are the parts of a sacrament? How do they that worthily communicate in the Lord's Supper feed upon the body and blood of Christ? How are they that receive the sacrament of the Lord's Supper to prepare themselves before they come unto it? What is the duty of Christians after they have received the sacrament of the Lord's Supper? The ministers of another day dealt with just such themes.

The minister cannot rightly prepare to lead his people in such acts of preparation and dedication without bringing his own life under the scrutiny of the white light of the holiness of God. He is about to stand in Christ's place. His hands are about to break the bread and raise the cup. He is about to speak Christ's words. How can he do this great service without purity of hand and heart? The frequency of the service is apt to forge fetters upon his faith. Responsibility for its proper administration, arrangements, and details fills his mind. It becomes him to keep watch over his own soul, to say to himself: " I am an ambassador on behalf of Christ. God has given to me this ministry of reconciliation."

XI. The First Communion

THE Christian Church from the very beginning has been under obligation faithfully to instruct in the Christian faith all who have sought communicant membership. This instruction was given ordinarily before baptism, but the making of a Christian proved to be a long and continuous process, and instruction was found to be necessary even after entrance into Church fellowship. The Christian faith had to be interpreted and enforced. The disciples themselves had been prepared in the school of Christ. Paul, after his baptism in Damascus under Ananias, in the silence of Arabia and in Jerusalem advanced in the knowledge of Christ. In his epistles he repeatedly speaks of the eagerness with which he sought to establish, comfort, and edify those whom he had won to Christ. Indeed, it was for this purpose the epistles were written, and scholars have discovered direct references in the New Testament to courses of formal instruction. The author of The Epistle to the Hebrews, for example, sums up such instruction under six heads: " repentance from dead works," " faith toward God," "teaching of baptisms," " laying on of hands," " resurrection of the dead," " eternal judgment." [1] Luke tells us that Theophilus was carefully " instructed " in the Gospel. [2] He informs us that Apollos was " instructed in the way of the Lord." [3] As the Church grew and multiplied, the task of instruction became heavy and assistants were necessary, so that the apostles should not be diverted from this important work. The Church would be wise today if its ministry should follow the same course, and see to it that nothing interferes with the task of instructing children, youth, and adults in Christian faith and life. In the Church, Paul tells us that Christ " gave some to be apostles; and some, prophets; and some, evangelists; and some, pastors and teachers; for the per-

fecting of the saints, unto the work of ministering, unto the
building up of the body of Christ." [4] It should be noted that
the term " pastors and teachers " refers to the same person.
He is the resident minister. While apostles, prophets, and
evangelists may minister in distant places, the " pastors and
teachers " minister in one locality. Their function is that of
shepherding, oversight, and instruction. The pastor, even in
our day, is the appointed teacher, and when he surrenders this
God-given function to someone else, he is doing a disservice
to the Church of Christ.

As time passed the instruction became more definite. The
Didache, or " Teaching of the Twelve," which was written
for the guidance of Gentile Christians, has been called the first
Christian manual of instruction. It was in use for several
centuries and throws a clear light upon the type of teaching
given. Teaching was moral and ethical rather than doctrinal,
and this can be understood when we remember the social conditions out of which new converts came. They belonged in
a pagan social order where immorality was common and purity,
such as Christianity demanded, was unknown. The New
Testament abounds in evidence that points to the terrible struggle through which early Christians passed in order to maintain those lovely Christian virtues which are the fruit of the
Spirit. " Be not deceived," writes Paul to the Corinthians:
" neither fornicators, nor idolaters, nor adulterers, nor effemi-
nate, nor abusers of themselves with men, nor thieves, nor
covetous, nor drunkards, nor revilers, nor extortioners, shall
inherit the kingdom of God. *And such were some of you.*" [5]
The need for clear, ethical instruction is everywhere recognized in the New Testament as it is in mission fields today.
Later the emphasis was placed upon doctrine and the formula
known as the Apostles' Creed gradually developed. The
growth of heretical teaching also made necessary the formu-
lation of New Testament doctrine and teaching.

It is clear that even in apostolic times adequate preparation
for baptism and Church membership could not be accom-

plished before baptism. Many who confessed their faith were immediately baptized and afterward instructed. Those who were converted on the Day of Pentecost were baptized and received into the Christian fellowship, but their knowledge of Christian truth must have been very inadequate. The Ethiopian, whom the Evangelist Philip met in the desert, was baptized after meager instruction. Events moved so fast that no fixed or ordered procedure was possible. Indeed it is seldom possible, for the way into the Kingdom of God is as varied as the personalities of men, and it is inevitable that, as in the Early Church, instruction must be continued after definite confession of faith in Christ. One of the failures of the modern Church is that young people are received to their first Communion and Christian instruction thereupon is concluded. Instead of baptism or confirmation being the goal and end, it should be the beginning of training in Christian character and conduct.

In the Early Church the instruction of catechumens was the chief task of the Church. It is still the first task in the foreign missionary field, and unless it is done adequately there is failure and breakdown. It should be the consistent policy of every Church, and then we would not be faced with an uneducated Church membership. Indeed, many of the people of our Churches are so religiously illiterate that they cannot express, much less propagate, the faith they profess. Anyone who has intimate knowledge of the student mind is bewildered with the lack of adequate Christian knowledge. Even among young people whose ideals and convictions are thoroughly Christian this is true. Throughout the Church there is a crying necessity for teachers capable of carrying on the work of instruction among children and young people. Largely for this reason there is discouragement on the part of ministers when they regard seriously the work being done in Sunday Schools and so-called discussion groups. We are paying the penalty first of neglect and then of having no definite course of instruction. The catechetical method has been surrendered.

Perhaps this was inevitable, but for lack of it we have inherited confusion and concern. It may be true that mere memorization has little educational value. To the child who said, " But I dinna understand it," the Scottish minister made reply: " Ye're no meant to understand it. Ye're meant to larn it." Millions did " larn " it and when it fell into disuse no adequate substitute was found. The mere memorization without knowledge of what is memorized has been questioned and perhaps rightly, but there is a catechetical method which is not mere memorization. Furthermore, we must not overlook the fact of history concerning the results accomplished in the Reformed Churches through catechetical instruction in the years gone by. Catechisms are being prepared today in other than religious areas. We have catechisms in physics and dynamics and mechanics and physiology and architecture. In a city public library these are almost the only catechisms listed. The catechetical method has had a long and successful history and has its modern counterpart in famous radio-network programs. It came early into use in the Christian Church. Cyril of Jerusalem (A.D. 350) states that the articles of the Creed were formulated, phrase by phrase, to cover the entire Christian teaching. Augustine gives in catechetical form instruction required for baptism, stating that the time demanded for training was at first from two to three years, but later the period of Lent was considered sufficient.

The Church of tomorrow builds upon the Church of today, and unless there is intelligent training of the children of the Church we can hardly expect the harvest for which we pray. The position taken by Horace Bushnell nearly a hundred years ago outlines the true religious education program. " The child," he says, " is to grow up a Christian, and never know himself as being otherwise. In other words, the aim, effort, and expectation should be, not, as is commonly assumed, that the child is to grow up in sin, to be converted after he comes to a mature age; but that he is to open on the world as one that is spiritually renewed, not remembering the time when he went through a technical experience, but seeming rather to have loved what is good from his earliest years." [6] Therefore he says: " Religion never thoroughly penetrates life, till it becomes domestic. Like that patriotic fire which makes a nation invincible, it never burns with inextinguishable devotion till it burns at the hearth." [7]

Is any Church succeeding at this important task? If so, we should go to school to that Church and learn from it. The Roman Catholic Church, of course, has the advantage of carrying on a system of Christian instruction in parochial schools. The question can be raised therefore: Since this Church has the equipment and the program for instruction in Christian faith and life, does the parochial school produce a better product than the public school? The answer in the realm of character seems to be, " No." The Roman-Catholic-educated child is not a better child than the child who has been educated in the public-school system. In relation to Church loyalty, the answer is, " Yes." The Roman Church does succeed in creating Church loyalty that lasts through life, but in relation to life and conduct it cannot be said that the parochial-school system produces a higher type of citizen than the nonparochial school.

In preparation for their first Communion, the children of the Roman communion are required to follow a consistent and unchanging program. *The Catechism of Christian Doctrine for First Communicants* is a small pamphlet of some thirty-six pages. It begins with Prayers for Little Children, the Lord's Prayer, the Apostles' Creed, the Confession; Short Acts of Faith, Hope, Love, Contrition; Blessing Before Meals and Grace After Meals. The catechism contains fourteen lessons, each containing from eight to ten questions. They follow the following subjects: Creation, Sin, the Redeemer, the Passion, Resurrection and Ascension, the Descent of the Holy Ghost, the Church, the Commandments, Grace and the Sacraments, Baptism and Confirmation, the Holy Eucharist, Holy Communion, Penance, Contrition, Prayer.

The demands made upon children taking their first Communion call for a minimum of instruction, for they are received at the early age of seven. They are instructed that they must partake of the Holy Communion at least once a year, at Easter time, and that they must always fast after midnight preceding the Communion. This act of confirmation must not be delayed. Instruction, which is impossible at such an early age, must be given later. When the candidate is prepared, the bishop performs the rite of confirmation: " I sign thee with the sign of the Cross, and I confirm thee with the chrism of salvation, in the Name of the Father, and of the Son, and of the Holy Ghost."

Full and perfect knowledge of Christian doctrine, therefore, is not required of those received to their first Communion. In a personal letter, Father Coakley, of Sacred Heart Church, Pittsburgh, says: " The knowledge of his religion which is required in a child before he can make his first Communion is such as will enable him to grasp according to his capacity those mysteries of the faith which are necessary as means to salvation, and to distinguish between the bread of the Eucharist and ordinary material bread, so that he may come to the Holy Eucharist with a devotion proportionate to his years." The fact that the child has inadequate training in the Christian faith puts upon parents, confessors, teachers, and priests an inescapable responsibility. Continuing, Father Coakley says: " We try as much as possible to have the parents do the teaching at home; it is part of the spiritual obligation of parents. But we do not rely on that entirely, of course; hence day after day in our parish school we supplement the home teaching by religious instruction, taking it slowly and thoroughly, and this is done by the sisters in the classes, and is supervised by the parish priests, both pastors and assistant priests. As far as we can in these hectic days, we try to pin the responsibility back on the parents; hence the father in the last analysis is the one who is to decide whether the child is to make his first Communion, and we cannot overrule his de-

cision. If we think he is in error, and sometimes the father and
mother are somewhat rigoristic, we proceed to enlighten their
minds as to their duties; but this does not often occur, and we
usually find the best kind of co-operation, parents and clergy
and teachers in school being united in their decision as to the
proper instruction of the child." It is important to understand that the chief burden of instruction follows rather than
precedes the first Communion. It will be noted that as children grow to maturity more demands are made upon them as
to their knowledge of the faith. *The Catholic Catechism,*
edited by Cardinal Gasparri, is a large book of nearly five hundred pages. It is in three parts: first, questions for little children; second, questions for children who have made their first
Communion; third, questions for adults. Those who are interested in religious education would do well to acquaint themselves with this volume, prepared, not by lay educational spe-
cialists, but by the high dignitaries of the Church.

In the Protestant Episcopal Church the rite of confirmation
is essential to admission to full communicant membership.
No one may take Communion without being confirmed. In
a personal letter, Rev. Arthur B. Kinsolving, II, of Calvary
Episcopal Church, Pittsburgh, says: " There is a well-estab-
lished precedent in our Church that this regulation is to pro-
tect the Communion service from the participation of the im-
mature. It does not apply to members of other Christian
communions. Like many rules in our Church this is debated
between the high and the low. Confirmation and the first
Communion are usually conducted at the same time in confirmation classes. This preparation varies, but its main basis may
be found in the offices of instruction in our prayer book. The
catechism is still taught in certain Churches, but there are
many variations. When we have junior groups between the
ages of fourteen and twenty, of course the material is somewhat different from that for adult groups. For years I have
used Dr. George Hodge's book on the Episcopal Church, as
well as another most interesting discussion of our Church by

Dr. Atwater. There is no set official material. The rector may decide how long to prepare his candidates for confirmation. In my own experience I have always had a confirmation class in the Church School for the entire academic year. With adult groups I have had between six and ten discussion classes on some weekday evening. The instruction is given by a Church School teacher for the young group, until about ten weeks previous to confirmation, at which time I try to take the class myself. I have oftentimes had them come Saturday mornings for an hour as well as Sunday. It is considered best for the rector or one of the clergy to give confirmation instructions in order to give it the proper emphasis."

When the Offices of Instruction contained in *The Book of Common Prayer* are examined it will be found that the teaching of the first part includes the interpretation of Christian baptism, the Apostles' Creed, the Ten Commandments, and the Lord's Prayer. In the second part, instruction is given concerning the Church and the sacraments. In *The Book of Common Prayer* there is included a short catechism, which covers in general the same subjects treated in the Offices of Instruction. When the candidate is prepared, the rite of confirmation follows, according to the definite ritual of *The Book of Common Prayer*. It is conferred by the bishop, usually on Easter Day. The candidate is asked the simple and impressive question, "Do you promise to follow Jesus Christ as your Lord and Saviour?" After a consecration prayer, the candidate kneeling, the bishop laying his hands upon his head says: "Defend, O Lord, this thy Child with thy heavenly grace; that he may continue thine for ever; and daily increase in thy Holy Spirit more and more, until he come unto thy everlasting kingdom." It is a memorable and satisfying service.

Lutheran Churches are exceedingly careful in preparing for the first Communion, and the growth and strength of that Church would testify to the value of such painstaking instruction. During its long history the Lutheran Church has had a simple, definite, and unchanging standard for those seeking admission to the Holy Communion. In all catechetical classes Luther's Small Catechism has been the unchanging and un-challenged textbook used by pastors in preparing for confir-mation. There have been many supplementary guidebooks prepared to assist pastors, but they are all based upon the catechism. Unlike many other Protestant Churches which go their own way, each pastor using his own method and his own material, the Lutherans have tenaciously clung to Luther's catechism and have followed its method and its contents. It is important to notice that it does not use the catechetical method which demands exact memorization, word by word, but what has been called the " thetical " form. The thetical form provides that the answers to the questions shall be rather explanations and interpretations. The meaning is to be under-stood and may be expressed in other words. " Christian truth," says a Lutheran authority, " is not something to be brought forth from the mind of the child by means of questions, but something divinely revealed and hence *to be communicated* to the child, the most natural form in which to set it before him in a text-book is the *thetical*. Luther's catechism itself is, indeed, in the form of questions and answers. But his catechism is con-fessional as well as didactic, and its words, memorized by the catechumen, are to become a personal confession of faith. The explanations of a text-book, on the other hand, are not to be memorized, but are meant to aid the catechumen in grasping the *thoughts* of the catechism. For this purpose, the *thetical* form is better than the interrogative, because the explanation is not continually broken by questions, and is thus better adapted to give the catechumens a connected idea of the doc-trines taught." [8]

Luther's Small Catechism is very simple. It is not a system of theology. It deals, however, with both faith and life. It includes the text and the accompanying interpretation of the Apostles' Creed, the Lord's Prayer, the Sacraments of Bap-tism and the Lord's Supper, and instruction concerning Con-fession, Personal Prayer, and Christian Duties. After each

Commandment, each article of the Creed, each petition of the Lord's Prayer, each sacrament, the simple question is asked, " What does this mean? " and a short, simple, clear explanation is given. This course of instruction is given by the pastor. It is not committed to any lay person, and Lutheran theological seminaries, as a rule, include catechetical instruction in the Department of Practical Theology. Since this is the first and most important task of the Church, it is fitting that it should also be the first and most important task of the clergy. The course of instruction usually covers a period of two years, and the consistency with which it is followed has brought forth abundant fruit in the faith and fellowship of the Church. The charge which Luther first laid upon pastors has never been lifted. " Wherefore I beseech you in the Name of God," he wrote, in the preface to the catechism, " to have mercy on the people who are entrusted to your care, and to assist us in introducing the catechism among them, and especially among the young. And if any of you do not possess the necessary qualifications, I beseech you to take at least the following forms, and read them, word for word, to the people. . . . Let the preacher take the utmost care to avoid all changes or variations in the text and wording of the Ten Commandments, the Lord's Prayer, the Creed, the Sacraments. Let him, on the contrary, take each of the forms respectively, adhere to it, and repeat it anew, year after year. For young and inexperienced people cannot be successfully instructed, unless we adhere to the same text or the same forms of expression. They easily become confused, when the teacher at one time employs a certain form of words and expressions, and, at another, apparently with a view to make improvements, adopts a different form. The result of such a course will be, that all the time and labor which we have expended will be lost. This point was well understood by our venerable fathers, who were accustomed to use the same words in teaching the Lord's Prayer, the Creed, and the Ten Commandments. We, too, should follow this plan when we teach these things, particularly in

the case of the young and ignorant, not changing a single
syllable, nor introducing any variations when, year after year,
we recur to these forms and recite them anew before our
hearers. Choose, therefore, the form of words which best
pleases you, and adhere to it perpetually." [9]

In Congregational and Methodist Churches the preparation
of candidates for baptism and confirmation is in the hands of
the pastor and varies with his interest in this important subject. The Methodist Church states that " all persons seeking
to be saved from their sins and desiring to live the Christian life
are eligible for membership." The pastor is obligated to instruct " all persons offering themselves for Church membership in the principles of the Christian life, in the baptismal and
membership vows and in the rules and regulations of the
Methodist Church." The instruction given depends largely
upon the instructor, and textbooks prepared by individuals are
generally in use. The pastor decides when and by whom the
instruction is to be given, and for what period of time. Three
ritual forms for reception of members are prescribed: one
for preparatory members, one for children, and one for full
membership. The confession of faith for full membership
takes place in the presence of the congregation in response to
the following questions: " Do you here in the presence of God
and this Congregation renew the solemn promise and vow that
was made at your Baptism? Do you confess Jesus Christ as
your Saviour and Lord and pledge your allegiance to His kingdom? Do you receive and profess the Christian faith as contained in the New Testament of our Lord Jesus Christ? Will
you be loyal to the Methodist Church, and uphold it by your
prayers, your presence, your gifts, and your service? " [10] Having made this confession, the candidate kneeling, the minister
lays his hands upon his head, saying: " The Lord defend thee
with His heavenly grace and by His Spirit confirm thee in the
faith and fellowship of all true disciples of Jesus Christ.
Amen." [11] The note of loyalty to the Methodist Church in

particular is noticeable in the ritual, as such denominational commitment is absent from the order in other Communions.

Churches of the Presbyterian and Reformed tradition have an inheritance of Christian instruction which has given them strength and influence in Church and State. The Westminster Directory for Worship gives these specific instructions:

" Children, born within the pale of the visible Church, and dedicated to God in baptism, are under the inspection and government of the Church; and are to be taught to read and repeat the Catechism, the Apostles' Creed, and The Lord's Prayer. They are to be taught to pray, to abhor sin, to fear God, and to obey the Lord Jesus Christ. And when they come to years of discretion, if they be free from scandal, appear sober and steady, and to have sufficient knowledge to discern the Lord's body, they ought to be informed it is their duty and their privilege to come to the Lord's Supper. The years of discretion in young Christians cannot be precisely fixed. This must be left to the prudence of the session. When persons baptized in infancy are to be admitted to full communion with the Church, they shall be examined as to their knowledge and piety, and shall in ordinary cases, with the approval of the session, make a public profession of their faith, in the presence of the congregation." [12]

It will be noticed from the wording of this statement that the instruction children and youth are to receive is to be given through the normal and regular channels of the Church. There is no call for communicant classes because the teaching is received during the whole period of childhood, and thus when children come to " years of discretion " and " have sufficient knowledge to discern the Lord's body," they are to be informed of their duty to confess Christ publicly, and partake of the Lord's Supper. For many years this was the procedure in the Churches. The Larger Catechism, and especially the Shorter Catechism, was the textbook for all Presbyterian children, and in like manner the *Heidelberg Catechism,* perhaps the most attractive of Reformation documents, was used in the Reformed Church of the Dutch and German traditions. These documents, like Luther's catechism, became the unvarying texts of instruction, and produced a Church membership that possessed competency of religious knowledge and Church loyalty. There are still communities in which this inheritance prevails. In some localities in America the Reformed Church still maintains parochial schools. Classes in religious instruction are held daily throughout the year, and carefully prepared textbooks compiled after the question-and-answer method, covering the Christian teaching concerning the Bible, the Creed, the Church, and Christian conduct, are in use. The theological atmosphere has changed in our day; because of this, and also on account of the opinion that memorization of statements of Christian truth beyond the comprehension of children is not good pedagogy, the use of the catechism has been largely abandoned. This setting aside of a uniform, authoritative system, without substituting another and a better one, has led to confusion. Every pastor introduces his own material and his own method. He may even possess no method. Numerous treatises have been published, many of them excellent, but they lack denominational acceptance. Sometimes the task of conducting communicant classes is committed to lay teachers and to directors of religious education, and such classes are carried on for four or six weeks, often during the Lenten period. The instruction given in this way should not be discounted, for frequently it is of a high order, but the criticism stands that it is on the whole inadequate, unequal, and fails in giving adequate knowledge of Christian truth, and in creating a common Church consciousness, without which no Church can maintain itself in strength and influence. This is a matter of such paramount importance that no pastor can measure up to his responsibility without the co-operation of his brethren. The situation demands a commitment of the Church to a definite, common course of instruction that can be maintained throughout a long period of years.

When the pastor and the Church session are satisfied with the qualification of those seeking to partake of their first Communion, the latter are received by the Church session and afterward publicly welcomed into Church membership. These or similar questions are asked of each candidate to be confirmed: "Do you here, in the presence of God and of this congregation, confess Christ as your Lord, and adhere to that Christian faith wherein you were baptized?" "Do you promise with God's help to serve the Lord, and keep His commandments all the days of your life?" "Now desiring to be received to the Lord's Supper, do you promise to make diligent use of the means of grace, giving your whole heart to the service of Christ and His kingdom in the world, and continuing in the peace and fellowship of the people of God?" These questions having been answered, the minister laying his hand, if such be his discretion, upon the head of each one in order kneeling before him, says: "Defend, O Lord, *this* Thy *Child* with Thy heavenly grace; that *he* may continue Thine for ever; and daily increase in Thy Holy Spirit more and more, until *he* come unto Thy everlasting kingdom. Amen." [13] This is the Order of Confirmation of Baptismal Vows.

It is evident that there is great need for improvement in this important task of training an intelligent Church membership. This can be brought about if the minister will make it his personal task. It will require adequate preparation, and also the setting apart of a period during the week when this work can be done. It may be found that Saturday morning, or some hour during Sunday, may be the best time. Any plan is better than no plan, and nothing can be accomplished without concentration. There is abundant material available and a few suggestions may be made.

The Protestant Episcopal Church has available *The Book of Common Prayer*, which provides the catechism and the Offices of Instruction, the emphasis being placed upon the Commandments, the Church, and the sacraments. These courses should be supplemented by the minister.

The Lutheran Church, as has been already stated, has made what it considers adequate provision. It has Luther's Short Catechism upon which various commentaries are available. There is also provided a very attractive study book on the liturgy of the Church, bearing the title *An Explanation of the Common Service*. It is worthy of study by those interested in preparing an intelligent Church membership.

The United Church of Canada has made great progress in this field. A well-prepared catechism for children has recently been published, and it has been favorably received and welcomed by the Church. Professor John Dow, of Emmanuel College, has done a noteworthy service in his exposition of the Statement of Faith of the United Church of Canada. It bears the title *This Is Our Faith*, and is an adequate exposition of the Creed of the Church in everyday language. No better compendium of the faith can be found.

The Presbyterian Church in the U. S. A. has made available *The Intermediate Catechism*, an admirable guide for communicant classes, and also an exposition of the Short Statement of the Reformed Faith under the title *A Manual of Faith and Life*. This book covers the essential facts of Christian doctrine in simple language, and has even found its way into theological seminaries. There is also provided a treatise, *My First Communion*, containing the ritual of the sacraments and an interpretation of the Church and the Christian life. In this connection it must be said that the Shorter Catechism is of inestimable value. The minister may use his own discretion where there should be modification and where there should be emphasis. It exalts the sacraments, the law of God, and the way of prayer. The minister who sets himself firmly to train the coming generation in the knowledge of Christian truth will not only provide for the vitality of the Church of tomorrow but will nourish his own soul.

Those who instruct children and youth in Christian life should always remember that education can never be a substitute for what the Scriptures call regeneration. Religious education, or education in religion, may miserably fail if the mysterious, miraculous work of the Holy Spirit is obscured or set aside. The Spirit does not work at the command of men, and the recognition of what the New Testament calls " the new birth " is essential in all true Christian training and instruction. Because we have thought we could do this task ourselves; because we have thought that the imparting of truth is the imparting of the Spirit of Christ; because we have taken it for granted that knowledge of Bible truth is equivalent to knowing God, we have often failed. If a person, even a little child, has by the working of God's Spirit been brought into a living faith and a confident trust in Christ, his Saviour, this is all the preparation he needs to break the bread and take the cup. The task of further instruction in Christian faith and life should indeed continue, not only for children, but for all of us, " till we all attain unto the unity of the faith, and of the knowledge of the Son of God, unto a fullgrown man, unto the measure of the stature of the fulness of Christ." [14]

XII. Preaching on the Sacraments

THE sacraments are the visible word of God. They have the same office as that of the Scriptures, which is to present Christ. In reading the Word of God we hear the message of salvation. In partaking of the Sacrament " Christ and the benefits of the new covenant are represented, sealed, and applied to believers." In the sacraments we see the Gospel. The sermon may fail. The hymns may fail. But the Sacrament silently proclaims the facts of the Christian faith. In speaking of the Lord's Supper Paul says, " As often as ye eat this bread, and drink the cup, ye *proclaim* the Lord's death." The word proclaim is καταγ-γέλλετε, " herald, preach." " The ordinance is a *verbum visibile*, a ' preaching ' of the entire Church in silent ministry." [1] The sacraments are indeed silent ministries and proclaim a full and complete Gospel of redemption.

It may be for this reason that preaching about the sacraments is more rare than it otherwise would be. An examination of volumes of modern sermons will convince even a cursory reader that this great theme suffers from neglect. The sacrament of baptism is rarely interpreted, while the sacrament of the Lord's Supper seldom receives from the pulpit the exposition which was customary in earlier days. In an old volume by James W. Alexander, entitled *Sacramental Discourses,* there are to be found sermons bearing such titles as these: " The Hymn of the Eucharist," " Communion in Christ's Body and Blood," " Christ's Death the Cardinal Doctrine." They contain teaching content.

The sacrament of baptism is rarely interpreted by modern preachers. Perhaps the truth therein contained is taken for granted or the theme is found too difficult. Even Alexander Maclaren, the prince of Baptist preachers, has nothing to say on those great texts which speak of the believer being " buried with him in baptism." The index to Joseph Parker's *The People's Bible* reveals only cursory references to the subject, and one fails to find a satisfactory interpretation of the ordinance. Among the immortal sermons of Frederick W. Robertson, however, we find that on two successive Sundays he dealt with the subject of baptism in an exhaustive manner, interpreting the Roman, the Calvinist, the Anglican view, and making application of the doctrine to life and character. It is pulpit teaching at its best. It is not necessary to agree with all he says, but such preaching reveals a seriousness of treatment lacking in our day.

The preacher has rich material awaiting his attention in the ritual for the administration of baptism. There is, first of all, the *Significance of Baptism*. The symbolism, as set forth, may be that of cleansing, purification, renewal, or burial and resurrection, dying unto sin and living unto righteousness. Ultimately the symbolism leads to the same conclusion. Baptism signifies a new life in Christ. It speaks of cleansing from sin, regeneration, resurrection unto life. It proclaims the fact that if any man is in Christ he is a new creature, and what Gospel theme needs to be proclaimed more than this? It is the central theme of grace. " Except one be born of water and the Spirit, he cannot enter into the kingdom of God. That which is born of the flesh is flesh; and that which is born of the Spirit is spirit. Marvel not that I said unto thee, Ye must be born anew." The pulpit needs to recover some of the big words it has lost. It has been losing the word " conversion," and the bond market has taken it up. It has been letting slip the word " redemption," and the bankers have laid hold of it. It has been obscuring the phrase " the new birth," and the biologists have been discovering it. Professor Simpson says of Principal Robert Rainy that his religious experience " was not so much a reaction as a realization — that equally genuine type of conversion (though the word conversion seems inappropriate to describe it) which consists in the love and grace of God in Jesus Christ becoming, and that perhaps not at any special time but with the natural development of mind and heart and will, something personal and something vital. A Christian life thus originated is at once supernatural and normal." [2] Baptism is rightly interpreted when it symbolizes the new life in Christ.

In the second place, there is the *Obligation of Baptism* resting upon parents or sponsors. Herein lies the true theological basis for Christian education. Let the words of a student of psychology speak in relation to this vital subject. " No greater disservice," says Robert F. Horton, " was ever done to religion than that officious undertaking of the Church to relieve the parents of their primary duties. The Church has no power to impart a true religion to infants and little children. By claiming that she has such a power, first at the font and then in the schools, she weakens the responsibility of those to whom that power necessarily appertains. Her function may be to inculcate the parental duty of teaching children, and even to instruct parents in the best methods of performing their task. She should be instant in season and out of season in reminding every father that he is by the very nature of the case compelled to teach his child from day to day the laws of the spiritual life, the claims of the Christian Gospel, the way by which the claims are to be recognised and the laws are to be obeyed. If the Church succeeds in rousing the father to a sense of his duty, she has succeeded with the child. But if she has relieved the father of his duty, she has injured not only the child but the father also. Amid the idle clamour that has filled the air in recent times about the religious education of the children, this primary truth has seldom or never been heard." [3] Continuing he says, " The father is as much bound to train the child-soul as he is to feed and clothe its body, and when once the Church begins to insist upon this truth, and when the State declines to give that religious instruction which only parents can give, every man will wake up to the reality of the situation, and will find that if he does not teach his children religion they will go without it, and that to leave his children without it is to inflict on them the cruellest wrong that man can perpetrate." [4]   These are strong words, but they point to the same emphasis as is evident in the administration of the sacrament of baptism, which pledges parents to bring up their children " in the nurture and admonition of the Lord."   Here is put into the hands of every minister an appropriate approach to a subject which merits the attention of the modern Church.   Here is the place to face the problems of juvenile delinquency and religious illiteracy.

Furthermore, there is the *Responsibility of Baptism,* resting squarely upon the Church.   Written into one of the more recent rituals of infant baptism is this pledge: " This Child is now received into Christ's Church: And you the people of this Congregation in receiving this Child promise with God's help to be *his* sponsor to the end that *he* may confess Christ as *his* Lord and Saviour and come at last to His eternal Kingdom. Jesus said, Whoso shall receive one such little child in my name receiveth me."   In this promise there is the recognition that the real sponsor of the baptized child is the congregation. Christian baptism takes place in Christ's Church, and it is into Christ and into membership of Christ's Church that the baptized person, infant or adult, is incorporated.   This places upon the Church, together with the parents, responsibility for the religious training of the child.   Dr. Horton, in the statement already quoted, places the primary emphasis upon the home, and this is unquestionably right, but the Church too has responsibilities, and here the preacher has a theme that is most timely.   He asks his people, in his sermons, questions such as these: Is the religious education carried on in this Church adequate?   Does the teaching measure up to the best standards? Does this Church support the training of its children and its youth as worthily as it supports its pulpit or its music?   In the light of present-day needs we know what the answer must be. One of the questions asked of the sponsors in the ritual of holy baptism in the Protestant Episcopal Church is this: " Having now, in the name of this Child, made these promises, wilt thou also on thy part take heed that this Child learn the Creed, the Lord's Prayer, and the Ten Commandments, and all other things which a Christian ought to know and believe to his soul's health? " [5]   The Church, as the true sponsor of every baptized child, should see that these same obligations are met, that the child learn the doctrines of the Christian faith " and *all other things which a Christian ought to know and believe to his soul's health."*   What a wealth of preaching material lies enshrined in such an obligation!

And then there is in the sacrament of baptism the *Promised Blessing of the Holy Spirit.*   In the sacrament, God the Father is at work; Christ is at work; the Holy Spirit is at work.   We baptize into " the Name of the Father, and of the Son, and of the Holy Spirit."   It is not man's act.   It is God's act.   If anywhere, then here, religion is set forth as a " given " thing, and the preacher misses everything when he fails to set forth God's activity both in His Word and in His sacraments.   One of our best psychologists has written some brave words on this subject.   He is speaking of the lack of power within the Christian Church, and he says that " this want of inspiration and power is associated with the fact that men no longer believe in the existence of the Spirit in any effective practical way.   They believe in God the Father, and they are reverent; they believe in the Son, and the Church numbers amongst its members millions who humbly try to ' follow in His steps '; but for all practical purposes they are like that little band at Ephesus who had ' not so much as heard whether there be any Holy Ghost,' and, lacking the inspiration of such a belief, they are weak and wonder why." [6]   Ringing through the New Testament is the constant promise, " He shall baptize you in the Holy Spirit."   This subject calls for reiterated emphasis.

The absence of great preaching on the subject of baptism is apparent to those who have searched the sermon files of the great preachers.   The situation is better in regard to the interpretation of the Lord's Supper.   There is usually to be found among the masters at least one comprehensive sermon on the

Eucharist, and every minister who has preached to the same congregation over a period of years must have gathered much material on this great theme. In the sermons of a long pastorate in the same Church, these sacramental subjects appear: " The Sacramental Evangel "; the text, " This do in remembrance of me." " The World's Greatest Sermon "; the text, " Ye proclaim the Lord's death." " The Spell of the Cross "; the text, " Who did bewitch you, before whose eyes Jesus Christ was openly set forth crucified." " The Guest Chamber "; the text, " Where is my guest-chamber? " " Christ the Bread of Life "; the text, " I am the bread of life." " The Eucharistic Feast "; the text, " When he had given thanks." " The Sacrament of Life "; the text, " This is my body, which is broken for you." " Our Lord's Sacramental Claim "; the text, " He that eateth this bread shall live forever." " The Second Crucifixion "; the text, " They crucify to themselves the Son of God afresh." " The Guests of God "; the text, " Thou preparest a table before me." " Sacramental Simplicity "; the text, " Come unto me, all ye that labor." " The Upper Room "; the text, " Let not your heart be troubled." " The Sacramental Invitation "; the text, " Drink ye all of it." " Memory and Hope "; the text, " This do . . . till he come." " Bread and Water "; texts: " I am the bread of life." " The water that I shall give." " The Sacramental Hymn "; the text, " When they had sung an hymn." " Sacrifice and Song "; the text, " When the burnt-offering began, the song of the Lord began also." " The Sacrament and the Gospel "; the text, " Ye proclaim the Lord's death till he come." Of course there is repetition, but there is no wandering from the central theme.

Taking for his text the familiar words, " This do in remembrance of me," Alexander Maclaren begins by stating that the account of the institution of the Lord's Supper in First Corinthians is older than any of the Gospel records. He divides his sermon, as usual, into three sections: (1) The Lord's Supper is a memorial of the past, and in this part of the sermon the emphasis is on the personal pronoun *me*. (2) It is a symbol for the present. The Christian life is not merely the remembrance of a historical Christ, but the present recognition of a living Christ. (3) It is a prophecy. The emphasis here is on the words, " Till I come." A memorial, a symbol, a prophecy — and interpreting the symbol he sets forth in strong language the Zwinglian position. Here is preaching, and here also is teaching.

The sermons of Phillips Brooks have little that bear upon the sacraments. There is a characteristic sermon entitled " Christ the Food of Man "; the text, " How can this man give us his flesh to eat? " It is an exposition, in the bishop's best style, of that great sacramental passage in John's Gospel. There is a long introduction, much too long for our day, in which he discusses the striving after real faith, and the answer given is: " I cannot *tell* you how. . . . Go and *do* it." Then he passes to the idea that food is for strength: inward as well as physical strength is needed, and this food of the soul is Christ. " The flesh was the expression of the human life of Jesus." Immediately the idea of the Sacrament is introduced, and he closes with the doctrine of the cross. It is preaching after the style that readers of Phillips Brooks know well, but it is not the direct preaching required in our day.

In a few brief words the sacramental approach of other great preachers may be set forth. Dr. Marcus Dods, scholar and preacher, takes the text, " This do in remembrance of me," using the same words for the title. He begins by pointing out our Lord's great simplicity. We are to remember Christ and be thankful. First, it was a kindness to his disciples to give them something to *do*. Secondly, he gave them something to do which would renew their remembrance daily. He chose the symbol of food. Thirdly, he bade them remember him in his death. He desired to be remembered in the hour of his deepest humiliation.

Dr. James Denney has a great sermon on " The Ideal Church "; the text, " They continued stedfastly in the apostles' teaching and fellowship, in the breaking of bread and the prayers." Here are four great themes: The Teaching, The Fellowship, The Breaking of Bread, The Prayers. The treatment suggests that the subject of the Sacrament may be treated as part of a larger whole, in this case the Church. The Sacrament was never far away from the mind of Alexander Whyte. He was a sacramental preacher. One of his sermons is called, " The Hebrew Child's Question at the Passover Supper," and his text, " It shall come to pass, when your children shall say unto you, What mean ye by this service? that ye shall say, It is the sacrifice of Jehovah's passover." He begins by picturing a Hebrew home. Then he speaks of the Passover and the Christian names — the Lord's Supper, the Communion, the Eucharist, the Lord's Table — with appropriate interpretations of each of the names, and closes with the thought that at the holy table Christ gave the disciples the new Commandment.

Alexander MacColl, in his fine book *The Sheer Folly of Preaching,* has a Communion address with no title and no text. He takes three simple words from the words of institution and explains them as they are related to the Sacrament. " Take ": The Church is forever asking men to give. Here Christ is asking men to take. " Do ": He does not ask us to feel, or even to think, but to do. " Show ": The world needs to be shown Christ. Said a young Indian, " Jesus Christ is hopelessly handicapped by his association with the West." We keep the forms but fail to show Jesus Christ to men.

Sacramental preaching does not require that the entire sermon should deal with some phase of the sacraments. It can be introduced, as in Dr. Denney's fine sermon, as part of a larger theme. Teaching about baptism and the Lord's Supper may be introduced appropriately in the sermon at any time, if the subject or the occasion requires it. The occasions when preaching on the sacraments is appropriate must be determined by the minister. It will be well, however, that he have some definite plan to follow. If it is his custom to keep the Church year, occasions will arise naturally when the sacraments become fitting subjects. In Churches where Communion is celebrated once a week, or once a month, then a special Sunday or Sundays should be set apart for this purpose. In Churches where the sacraments of infant baptism and the Lord's Supper are administered every three months, those occasions would be appropriate for sacramental instruction. This above all: Let the minister have a plan and remain faithful to it. The library, consisting of books on what and how to preach, has grown in our day to amazing proportions. There are books in this library by the masters. There is advice on all subjects pertaining to the ministry, but there is an absence of worth-while discussions on the place of the sacraments in the life of the Church, and little counsel is given about how to educate a congregation upon their message and mission.

There is, however, no lack of literature which interprets the sacrament for the laity. The very excellent and beautifully printed *An Explanation of the Common Service* is a popular exposition of the Lutheran order of Holy Communion. The book has been in use for many years and has been repeatedly revised. It is dedicated " To the young Lutheran who asks the meaning of the Beautiful Liturgy of his Church." It gives in red the words of the Liturgy and after each separate section, in question and answer form, the interpretation. The entire service is explained, with the result that those who study it, and those to whom the contents are given through preaching, become intelligent Lutheran communicants. Similar efforts to interpret other rituals have been made. *The Book of Common Order* of the Church of Scotland and *The Book of Common Prayer* have been interpreted for lay readers. In all such treatises the preacher will find a wealth of material from which he can draw, for the movements within the framework of the orders for the administration of the Lord's Supper have much in common. The introductory words to the service of Holy Communion in *The Book of Common Worship* gather up what is common to all such services and provide an incomparable guide for preaching: " As we draw near to the Lord's

Table to celebrate the Holy Communion of the Body and Blood of Christ, we are gratefully to remember that our Lord instituted this Sacrament — For the perpetual memory of His dying for our sakes and the pledge of His undying love; as a bond of our union with Him and with each other as members of His mystical Body; as a seal of His promises to us and a renewal of our obedience to Him; for the blessed assurance of His presence with us who are gathered here in His Name; and as a pledge of His coming again." [7]

XIII. Is Inter-Communion Possible?

" THAT they may find unity," is the common prayer of the Protestant Churches in our day. It is with this passionate desire that many look to the World Council of Churches and to the Ecumenical Movement with new hope. This desire for unity is closely bound up with the observance of the sacrament of the Lord's Supper. When Christians from all the Churches and from all lands meet in conference to consider the subject of Church unity, there is a deep desire that unity should find expression in the celebration of the Holy Communion in which all the delegates can participate. This, however, has not been possible. Separate sacramental services have been held, or no service, and the result has been disillusionment and regret.

For these reasons, in 1942 a commission was appointed in America to study the subject of inter-Communion in relation to the Ecumenical Movement.[1] This commission, of which the author was the chairman, was asked to find an answer to the question: When conferences and councils are gathered in the interests of unity, is it possible to celebrate the sacramental service so that all present may participate? On account of the war it was not possible to have the help of commissioners from the Continent, so the American commission confined its work to Church situations in the United States and Canada. The commission was made up of representatives of the following Churches: The Southern Baptist, the Northern Baptist, the Presbyterian Church in Canada, the Disciples of Christ, the Methodist, the Protestant Episcopal, the Presbyterian Church in the U. S. A., the Greek Orthodox, the Congregational-Christian, the Church of the Brethren, the United Lutheran, and the United Church of Canada. Since this subject is of increasing interest, especially in view of the formation of the World Council of Churches and the growing importance of the Ecumenical Movement, it is fitting to give the summary of the report formulated by the commission.

Frequently there is ambiguity in the use of the words " inter-Communion " and " open Communion " and it is necessary to define these terms. The formula agreed upon states: " By ' inter-Communion ' we understand full mutuality as between two or more Churches with respect to the ministers who may celebrate, as well as the members who may partake of, the Lord's Supper or Holy Communion; by ' open Communion ' we understand the extension by a given Church of the privilege of communicating to the members of another Church or Churches. Where ' open Communion ' is mutual, we have a form of limited ' inter-Communion,' but it is important not to confuse such limited intercourse with full ' inter-Communion.' "

It was necessary to secure all data available before entering upon conference and discussion. Two assignments, therefore, were given to the representatives on the commission. The first was a request for careful answers to a questionnaire prepared by the commission in plenary session setting forth the practice of each of the communions represented regarding inter-Communion and open Communion, and the basis for such practice. The second request was for a prepared statement, of not more than five hundred words, setting forth the beliefs held and the practice followed by the communions represented. There is, therefore, manifest duplication and overlapping; but the commission was able from the documents that came into its hands to frame a comprehensive report and make factual recommendations.

The questionnaire was as follows: " 1. What is required by your Church as to the officiating minister at the Lord's Supper? 2. Can others than ordained ministers so officiate? 3. A. What is the practice of your Church with regard to admission to the communicant membership (1) of children: (a) customary age? (b) preliminary requirements, such as baptism, instruction, confirmation, etc.? (c) method of admission (e.g., rite or ceremony)? (2) of other persons: (*a*) preliminary requirements, such as baptism, instruction, confirmation, etc.? (*b*) method of admission (e.g., rite or ceremony)? B. What are the rules and practice of your Church with regard to communicating at a particular observance of the Holy Communion? C. What are the rules and practice of your Church with regard to ' open Communion '? 4. How frequently is the Holy Communion customarily observed in your Church? 5. How does your Church connect the Holy Communion with God's grace? Is it a means of grace in a sense different from an ordinary service of worship? If so, how? 6. Is the primary emphasis of your Church upon its responsibility for the Holy Communion as necessary to the spiritual growth of its members or upon the Communion as an expression of the unity of the whole Body of Christ? 7. In what sense and to what extent does your Church regard the Lord's Supper as a memorial? Does it view this as sacrificial in character? 8. Do you regard the Holy Communion as a necessary ordinance: (*a*) for individual salvation? (*b*) for the existence of a Church? 9. Do you consider that there is any benefit in noncommunicating attendance at the Holy Communion? If so, what? "

In answer to the first and second questions — " What is required by your Church as to the officiating minister at the Lord's Supper? " and " Can others than ordained ministers so officiate? " — there is general agreement that ordination is required, although acute differences presented themselves. The Northern Baptist said, " The ordinance at which a layman officiates is equally valid "; the Southern Baptist, " In rare instances licensed preachers have been invited to officiate "; the Disciples of Christ, " Ordained elders also officiate "; the Methodist, " Normally one must be an ordained elder, but in country places occasional dispensation is given for a deacon "; the United Church of Canada, " Under the strictest supervision, certification may be granted to particular Home Mission Agents to administer both sacraments. But this is not to be regarded as affecting the regular practice of the Church; it is an adaptation to meet an abnormally difficult situation." On the other hand the Greek Orthodox demands valid ordination. The Protestant Episcopal's Low Church statement says, " He shall be a priest episcopally ordained "; and the High Church statement asserts, " He must be a priest ordained by a bishop of apostolic succession." The replies, therefore, to these first two questions present one acute situation with which the commission had to deal.

The third question is both comprehensive and critical. It relates to current practices and requirements for admission to communicant membership: first, as to children, and, secondly, as to other persons; to the rules and practices regarding communicating at a particular observance of the Holy Communion; and to the rules and practices relating to open Communion.

On the whole the Churches agree as to the appropriate time for admission to the Holy Communion. In general " early adolescence," with the ages ranging from twelve to sixteen years, is the period mentioned. The Southern Baptists, however, stated that " some are as young as seven years "; and the Greek Orthodox asserts, " All ages, beginning with babyhood." The Baptist and Disciples of Christ Churches admit by " baptism by immersion," while the other communions practice infant baptism and confirmation. The Presbyterian Churches receive baptized children on " confirmation of baptismal vows " and others by " baptism and public profession of faith in Christ." The Episcopal Church admits to the Holy Communion by " baptism and confirmation by a bishop."

There is a noticeable emphasis, on the part of all the Churches, upon proper instruction before reception to membership and confirmation. The Episcopal Church demands the " ability to say the Apostles' Creed, the Lord's Prayer, and the Ten Commandments plus instruction in the offices preceding Order of Confirmation." In many Churches communicant classes are held, which vary according to the standards of the Church and the ideals of the pastor.

The replies to cognate questions regarding the rules and practices of the Churches as to communicating at particular observances of the Holy Communion and the attitude toward open Communion present such a divergence of views that it is difficult to discover the way to unity and inter-Communion. It is necessary here to record the answers in some detail. Northern Baptist Churches " practice open Communion " and " issue a general invitation at the Church service for all who profess to believe in and follow the Lord Jesus Christ to partake of the Lord's Supper." Southern Baptist Churches state that there is " an increasing number of Southern Baptist Churches that practice open Communion of Christians, but many Churches still invite only ' those of like faith and order.' " The statement of the Church of the Brethren must be quoted: " There is a growing sentiment and practice in the Church of the Brethren toward open Communion, restricted however to those whose manner of life satisfies their Brethren acquaintances that they exhibit a quality of moral living sufficiently high and distinctive to be of Jesus Christ and not of the world — and so Brethren were willing to commune with them. This never takes the form of a broadcast public invitation to everyone to attend the Communion."

Open Communion is almost universally observed among the Disciples of Christ: " It is generally understood that members of other denominations are welcomed." The United Lutheran Church states that " open Communion is not favored as a general practice." The generally accepted rule is: " Lutheran pulpits for Lutheran ministers only. Lutheran altars for Lutheran communicants only. Exceptions to the Rule belong in the sphere of privilege and not of right." The Presbyterian Churches extend an invitation " in the most generous terms and this invitation has been interpreted by our General Assembly to refer to all members of evangelical Churches who may be present." The Methodist Church reports that " open Communion (while not *official*) is general. Those are invited who are seeking to ' follow the Lord Jesus Christ in sincerity and truth.' " The answer of the Greek Orthodox Church states that practice differs in the different national Churches. There are, however, definite rules in the Russian Orthodox Church such as fasting, prayers, meditation, abstinence from pleasures, confession, absolution, and bodily purity. " The Orthodox Church does not know the practice of the ' open Communion,' while rules exclude the very possibility of it." The Low Church statement of the Protestant Episcopal Church asserts that " there is no rule which regularizes open Communion, and the rubric at the end of the order of confirmation would, if literally interpreted, restrict the reception of Communion to confirmed persons. Many Episcopal bishops and priests, however, look upon this rubric as a rule of domestic discipline and ' open ' the Communion to baptized Christians of other communions who desire to come in repentance and faith." The High Church group of the Episcopal Church asserts that " according to the faith and practice of the undivided Catholic Church of the Fathers, to which Anglicanism has always appealed, no one is to be considered a member of the Church, in the full sense of the word, with the right to communicate at her altars, unless he has been validly baptized and validly confirmed, and is in union with his lawful bishop." The United Church of Canada invites " all who, having come to years of discretion, have made credible profession of faith in and obedience to the Lord Jesus," and such also is the position of the Congregational-Christian Church. From this analysis it is readily seen how difficult it is to reconcile the conflicting views. This conflict at the present time seems to be inescapable, and the judgment reached by the commission reflects this conclusion.

The remaining questions asked of the representatives of the Churches by the commission may be answered more briefly. To the inquiry, " How frequently is the Holy Communion customarily observed in your Church? " the replies are: Northern Baptists and Methodist, monthly; Southern Baptists, quarterly; Church of the Brethren, in the spring and fall; Disciples of Christ, weekly; Lutherans and Presbyterians, four to six times a year and on festivals; Greek Orthodox, daily, often weekly; Protestant Episcopal: first statement, " every week "; second statement, " every Sunday, in many parishes daily "; United Church of Canada, " three to twelve times a year."

The fifth question is theological: " How does your Church connect the Holy Communion with God's grace? Is it a means of grace in a sense different from an ordinary service of worship? If so, how? " Without calling the roll of the Churches, the answers vary in the same way as do the answers to the question concerning open Communion. Lutherans " believe it to be a veritable means of grace " and " different from an ordinary service of worship." The Greek Orthodox assert that " it is different from an ordinary service of worship. The union of the faithful with Christ and the indwelling in him of the Holy Spirit are mediated in the Holy Communion by the participation of the faithful in the ' divine meal,' not only morally, but physically, bodily; he is grafted on the ' true vine,' incorporated in Christ not allegorically but really; he is in Christ and Christ in him otherwise than outside the Holy Communion." The Protestant Episcopal Low Church statement asserts that the Holy Communion is " a principal means of grace " different from all other services; while the High Church statement affirms that " in the other sacraments we receive grace, but in the Eucharist we receive the very Author of grace in his body and blood, his soul and his divinity — all that he has and is."

No clear or particular answer was given to the question, " Is the primary emphasis of your Church upon its responsibility for the Holy Communion as necessary to the spiritual growth of its members or upon the Communion as an expression of the unity of the whole Body of Christ? " A similar idea is behind the question, " In what sense and to what extent does your Church regard the Lord's Supper as a memorial? Does it view this as sacrificial in character? " Most of the Churches respond by saying that the Lord's Supper is a memorial and not

a sacrifice. There are, however, Churches which while asserting the memorial nature of the Sacrament also emphasize its
sacrificial nature. The Lutheran reply says, " The commemoration of the Lord's Supper involves Eucharistic sacrificial elements of true worship, of praise and thanksgiving, of self-
dedication, high resolve "; the Presbyterian: " The memorial
is not ' a sacrifice,' but ' the memorial of Christ's sacrifice of
himself.' It involves our self-offering as we receive it, presenting ourselves a living sacrifice to him "; the Greek Orthodox: " It does view this as sacrificial in character. The redeeming death of Christ is understood to be a sacrificial act,
and this is, by extension, reproduced in the Holy Communion
where ' the Lamb of God . . . is sacrificed.' " The Low
Church Episcopal statement asserts, in the language of *The
Book of Common Prayer*, that it is " ' a perpetual memory of
that his precious death and sacrifice, until his coming again.'
It is sacrificial in the sense that through it the one oblation and
sufficient sacrifice of Calvary is dramatized, vivified, and
pleaded before God." The High Church statement of the
Episcopal Church holds that " it re-presents and presents to
the Father the body and blood of his Son, present on the altar
(no less than in the heavenly sphere) as priest and victim, once
slain, but alive forevermore, who pleads and presents his one
sacrifice finished on Calvary, but available forever, and applies
to our souls and to the whole Church, living and departed, the
benefits of his Passion."

As we would anticipate, various and very definite answers
are given to the question, " Do you regard the Holy Communion as a necessary ordinance: (*a*) for individual salvation?
(*b*) for the existence of a Church? " To the first inquiry the
Northern Baptist, the Southern Baptist, the Church of the
Brethren, and the Presbyterian replies say, " No." The Methodist Church, the Greek Orthodox, and the Protestant Episcopal say, " Yes." To the second inquiry the answer of the
Northern Baptist is, " No "; the answers of the other Churches
are, " Yes." To the question, " Do you consider that there is

any benefit in noncommunicating attendance at the Holy
Communion? If so, what?" the answers given are uniformly
in the affirmative, and the reasons given are: " It is educative ";
" A sense of spiritual fellowship "; " Spiritual impressions are
made "; " All the benefits that come normally from true worship "; " An incentive "; " A solemn and unusually effective
mode of presenting the claims of the Gospel "; " They share
in the experience of others." It is: " An aid to prayer, worship, and fellowship "; " Participation in the sacrifice of Calvary by impetration "; " A great religious occasion."

The documents presented by the representatives of the various Communions parallel the answers given to the questionnaire. The Northern Baptist and the Southern Baptist
Churches reveal a marked tendency to move from the position
of closed to open Communion: " Since faith, not baptism, according to the Baptist interpretation of the New Testament, is
the avenue of God's redeeming grace, every man of faith must
be allowed to commune. A man is to be accepted at the table
not by virtue of the validity of his baptism but by virtue of
the validity of his faith." " An increasing number of Southern Baptist ministers and Churches favor the free inter-Communion of Christians. They are convinced that there is no
adequate theological ground for close Communion." The
Disciples of Christ assert that " the Disciples are becoming
more liberal in their attitude toward members of other denominations who might wish to commune with them. There
are some who still say, ' We neither invite nor debar,' but there
is a growing tendency to invite all Christians." The Methodist
Church states that " there is no obstacle in Methodist law or
practice which stands in the way of inter-Communion on the
part of evangelical Christians either at regular services of the
Church or on special occasions." The Presbyterian Churches
hold fellowship " with all Churches which accept as essential
and fundamental the doctrinal basis adopted by the Federal
Council of the Churches of Christ in America, the Faith and
Order Movement, and the World Council of Churches." The

same practice is maintained in the United Church of Canada and the Congregational-Christian Church.

These same Churches would welcome the practice of inter-Communion in the Ecumenical Movement. There are other Churches, however, that hold a stricter view. The attitude of the Church of the Brethren is: " Were the news to be carried to the Annual Conference of the Church of the Brethren that all the rest of the Christian denominations had agreed to inter-Communion the news would probably be received in a coolly rational spirit, and the sentiment would be, ' We hope it does them good.' And it would not be hostility or indifference to denominational neighbors that would prompt this unenthusiastic reception." The Lutheran Churches present differing points of view: " Responsibility for admission to the altar rests not only with the minister, but also with individuals who desire to receive the Sacrament with their families or friends in Churches other than their own. Thus many pastors welcome non-Lutherans of whose Christian character and standing they have information. Some extend a general invitation. The groups, however, which freely did this a half century ago are now more guarded in their practice, while many conservative pastors are less rigid than formerly. All groups agree that indiscriminate inter-Communion is undesirable. Church unity cannot be artificially or mechanically forced. Inter-Communion is a goal and should not be used as a means."

The Protestant Episcopal Church presented two statements which show considerable differences in position. The Low Church statement is generously worded: " There is a wide divergence of practice within the Episcopal Church as to open Communion. Many bishops and priests habitually invite all Christian people who may be present to partake of the Sacrament. Others would favor departure from the normative practice of close Communion only under exceptional circumstances. Still others, probably a small minority, stand for rigid adherence to the confirmation rubric. As regards the participation of Episcopalians in the Communion services of other

Christian bodies, there is no rule.   Probably such participation is much less frequent than is the communication of non-Episcopalians at Episcopal altars."

The High Church group, however, interprets the position of the Church in stricter terms: "The principles of the ancient Church to which the whole Anglican communion has consistently appealed, utterly exclude non-Episcopal ordination, which was always treated as invalid, from the time that the threefold ministry emerged fully developed, into the light of history.   To communicate at altars served by such ministers would, for an instructed Churchman, be the sin of schism.   Intercelebration likewise at once obscures and condones the fact of schism — it hides the symptoms of the disease of disunity while the disease remains unhealed."

The statement of the Orthodox Greek-Catholic Eastern Churches sets forth the most extreme position presented to the commission: "The Orthodox Church regards herself as *the* Church of God, one, holy, catholic, and apostolic, keeping the Christian tradition unchanged since the earliest times, and having the divinely instituted priesthood and sacraments.   Her members form one body united by common faith, priesthood, and canonical structure.   Those individuals and communities that have departed from this faith, have priesthood of their own or live without any, and follow their own way of life, are the outsiders.   They are unto her ' as an heathen man and a publican '; there can be no religious communion with them until they repent."

From a perusal of these comments it is evident that, while there is a close bond of unity centering in the Holy Communion, there is also a very sharp division which is not personal but rooted in the faith and order of the Churches represented. Some Churches consider the Sacrament as a memorial symbol only; others hold that there is in the Sacrament the very spiritual presence of Christ; while others hold a sacrificial view. These distinctions are evident, not only in the answers given to the questions as presented, but also in the more elaborate statements prepared by the members of the commission. They reassert the positions put forward more briefly in the questionnaire.

The conclusions reached by the commission in answer to the mandate of the Continuation Committee " to consider the principles which should govern the practice of the Ecumenical Movement in regard to inter-Communion and open Communion " are unanimous but are not reassuring. There are some who hold that inter-Communion is a prerequisite to union, a means of promoting Christian unity, and an expression of an already existing spiritual unity. On the other hand, there are those who are opposed to inter-Communion in any form as a means to unity. They hold that inter-Communion is the final goal to which all our efforts are directed. Even so, there are those who would restrict the Holy Communion to baptized members of other Churches, while others would require baptism and confirmation in conformity with the order of their own Churches. There are those too who would confine the Holy Communion to those holding the faith of the Church under whose auspices the Sacrament is celebrated. Certainly there should be a note of contrition on the part of all communions as these statements and conclusions are presented. "Our studies, therefore," says the commission, "make it evident that both inter-Communion and full reciprocal open Communion are at present unattainable even within the bounds of the Ecumenical Movement." To many these are discouraging words, but since they are true words we will, by recognizing their validity, continue more surely to make progress toward the unity of the Church for which our Lord prayed and for which, following his example, we pray.

Notes

FOREWORD

1. *Our Faith*, p. 135.
2. *Credo*, pp. 200, 211.
3. *Christian Doctrine*, p. 157.

I

1. Acts 2:46.
2. Heb. 11:3.
3. P. 367.
4. Rom. 1:20.
5. Isa. 40:21–26.
6. Ps. 139:8–10.
7. II Cor. 4:18.
8. Rev. 21:15, 17.
9. Jeans, *The Mysterious Universe*, pp. 148, 149.
10. Longfellow, " Nature."
11. Masefield, " The Everlasting Mercy."
12. Dickens, *Christmas Books* (Everyman's Edition), p. ix.
13. Browning, " One Word More."
14. Acts 2:2, 3.
15. *The Institutes of the Christian Religion*, IV. xiv. 1.
16. Hunter, *The Teaching of Calvin*, p. 166.
17. Simpson, *The Evangelical Church Catholic*, p. 85.
18. The Shorter Catechism. Q. 85.
19. Rom. 4:11.
20. *The Epistle of Paul to the Romans*, pp. 63, 64.
21. *Op. cit.*, IV. xiv. 9.
22. MacLeod, *A Faith for Today*, p. 17.

II

1. Phil. 2:6, 7.
2. Lowell, " The Vision of Sir Launfal."

3. *The Apostolic Preaching and Its Developments*, p. 5.
4. Hunter, *The Unity of the New Testament*, p. 31.
5. *Our Faith*, pp. 127, 128.
6. *The Institutes of the Christian Religion*, IV. xviii. 19.
7. Donovan, *The Catechism of the Council of Trent*, p. 107.
8. *Ibid.*, p. 107.
9. *Ibid.*, p. 108.
10. Clarke, *Outline of Christian Theology*.
11. Calvin, *op. cit.*, IV. xiv. 17.
12. Ch. XXVIII, Sec. vi.
13. I Cor. 10:4.
14. John 6:51.
15. Acts 2:46.
16. Acts 2:42.
17. Rom. 16:16; I Cor. 16:20.
18. Ch. IX.
19. *Apologia*, I. 65.
20. *Ibid.*, I. 66.
21. Maxwell, *The Liturgical Portions of the Genevan Service Book*, p. 39.

III

1. Matt. 3:6.
2. Mark 1:4.
3. Luke 3:3.
4. John 1:31.
5. John 1:25.
6. Matt. 21:25.
7. Brilioth, *Eucharistic Faith and Practice, Evangelical and Catholic*, pp. 49, 50.
8. Ex. 30:18, 19.
9. Ezek. 36:25, 26.
10. Pp. 508, 509.
11. Matt. 3:11.
12. Major, Manson, and Wright, *The Mission and Message of Jesus*, p. 333.
13. Acts 19:2–5.
14. John 4:2.
15. John 3:5.
16. Westcott, *The Gospel According to St. John*, p. 50.
17. Matt. 28:18, 19.

18. Mark 16:15, 16.
19. *Op. cit.*, p. 250.
20. " The Synoptic Gospels," p. 340.
21. Ch. VII.
22. Acts 2:38.
23. Acts 8:16.
24. Acts 19:5.
25. Rom. 6:3.
26. Gal. 3:27.
27. I Cor. 6:11.
28. I Cor. 1:13.
29. Eph. 4:5, 6.
30. Gal. 3:27.
31. Col. 2:12.
32. Rom. 6:3.
33. Hoskyns, *Cambridge Sermons*, p. 28.
34. *Service Book*, pp. 274, 275.
35. *Confessions*, X. xxvii. 38.

IV

1. *The Encyclopædia Britannica* (Eleventh Edition), Vol. XXIII, p. 977.
2. *The Book of Common Worship*, p. 67.
3. *Service Book*, p. 278.
4. *Book of Common Worship*, p. 79.
5. *Book of Common Order*, p. 97.
6. *The Confession of Faith* . . . (1647), p. 294.
7. Harry Webb Farrington.
8. IV. xiv. 9.
9. 1901 Edition, p. 136.
10. Ch. XXVIII, Sec. vi.
11. Macleod, *Church, Ministry and Sacraments*, p. 81.
12. Stump, *An Explanation of Luther's Small Catechism*, p. 25.
13. Kerr, Hugh T., Jr., *A Compend of Luther's Theology*, p. 164.
14. Gasparri, *The Catholic Catechism* (348), p. 157.
15. Davidson, *The Meaning of Baptism*, p. 13.
16. *Op. cit.*, IV. xiv. 9.
17. *Ibid.*, IV. xv. 15.

V

1. Gal. 3:27.
2. P. 945.
3. *Ibid.*, p. 952.
4. *Ibid.*, p. 953.
5. *Ibid.*, p. 955.
6. Straton, *Baptists: Their Message and Mission*, p. 161.
7. *Apologia*, I. 61:1, 15.
8. *Against Heresies*, II. 22, 4.
9. Ep. 98, ad Bonifatium.
10. See Hastings, *Encyclopaedia of Religion and Ethics*, Vol. II, p. 393.
11. Council of Carthage, A.D. 418, Canon 2.
12. I Cor. 7:14.
13. Acts 10:44.
14. Acts 10:47, 48.
15. Acts 16:15.
16. Acts 16:33.
17. I Cor. 1:16.
18. Acts 3:25.
19. Hastings, *op. cit.*, Vol. II, p. 401.
20. Luke 18:15.
21. Matt. 19:13.
22. Matt. 19:14.
23. Cox, *The Bird's Nest*, p. 83.
24. Acts 1:8.
25. P. 31.
26. *Lectures on the Church and the Sacraments*, p. 166.
27. Deut. 6:4–7.

VI

1. *The Institutes of the Christian Religion*, IV. xv. 20.
2. Sec. 17.
3. Gasparri, *The Catholic Catechism* (352), p. 158.
4. Straton, *Baptists: Their Message and Mission*, pp. 43, 44.
5. Strong, *Systematic Theology*, Vol. III, p. 933.
6. Matt. 3:6.
7. Matt. 3:11.
8. Matt. 3:16.

9. John 3:23.
10. Acts 8:36, 38.
11. *Op. cit.*, IV. xv. 19.
12. Rom. 6:4.
13. Col. 2:12.
14. I Cor. 10:2.
15. *Epistles of St. Paul*, Vol. I, p. 291.
16. *Council of Trent*, II. ii. 17.
17. Ch. XXVIII, Sec. iii.
18. Moule, *Colossian Studies*, p. 152.
19. Mark 7:3, 4.
20. Luke 11:38.
21. Ch. VII.
22. Marucchi, *Manual of Christian Archeology*, p. 287.
23. Acts 15:28.
24. *Op. cit.*, IV. xv. 19.
25. *History of the Christian Church*, p. 123.
26. Gal. 5:1.

VII

1. Major, Manson, and Wright, *The Mission and Message of Jesus*, p. 776.
2. Jer. 31:31–33.
3. Heb. 7:18–25.
4. Heb. 9:18–20.
5. Heb. 9:13–15.
6. *The Catechism of the Council of Trent*, p. 156.
7. Barbour, *Life of Alexander Whyte*, p. 243.
8. *Ibid.*, p. 244.
9. *Ibid.*
10. Heb. 9:24–26.
11. Wotherspoon, *Religious Values in The Sacraments*, pp. 243, 244.
12. The Larger Catechism. Q. 170.
13. *The Institutes of the Christian Religion*, IV. xvii. 32.

VIII

1. I Cor. 5:7, 8.
2. *Epistulae*, X. 96.

3. I Cor. 11:20.
4. I Cor. 10:21.
5. Heb. 9:26.
6. *The Catechism of the Council of Trent*, p. 169.
7. I Cor. 10:16, 17.
8. Matt. 26:27.
9. Mark 14:23.
10. Clow, *The Church and The Sacraments*, p. 219.
11. *The Lord's Supper and The Liturgy*, p. 55.
12. *The Book of Common Prayer*, p. 82.
13. *Ibid.*, p. 83.
14. *Highways of the Heart*, p. 90.   A devotional book issued by The Board of Evangelism and Social Service, Wesley Buildings, Toronto.
15. Candlish, *The Sacraments*, pp. 89, 90.
16. *The Institutes of the Christian Religion*, IV. xiv. 17.
17. *The Book of Common Worship*, p. 67.
18. *Ibid.*, p. 68.
19. Luckock, *The Divine Liturgy*, pp. 303, 304.
20. Milligan, *The Ministry of Worship*, p. 113.
21. Gasparri, *The Catholic Catechism*, p. 165.
22. *The Confession of Faith* . . . (1647), p. 295.
23. *The Book of Common Worship*, p. 67.

IX

1. Kingsley, F., ed., *Charles Kingsley: Letters and Memories of His Life*, I, 154.

X

1. *The Confession of Faith* . . . (1647), p. 295.
2. Donovan, *The Catechism of the Council of Trent*, pp. 168, 169.
3. *Ibid.*, p. 169.
4. I Cor. 11:27–29.
5. The Larger Catechism. Q. 171.
6. The Fourth Book, Ch. I.
7. Ch. IX, Sec. vi.
8. *Religion on the American Frontier*, p. 63.

9. Smith, Joseph, *Old Redstone: or Historical Sketches of Western Presbyterianism, Its Early Ministers, Its Perilous Times, and Its First Records*, pp. 155, 156.

10. Mark 14:13–15.

11. *What to Preach*, p. 77.

XI

1. Heb. 6:1, 2.
2. Luke 1:4.
3. Acts 18:25.
4. Eph. 4:11, 12.
5. I Cor. 6:9–11.
6. *Christian Nurture*, p. 10.
7. *Ibid.*, p. 63.
8. Stump, *An Explanation of Luther's Small Catechism*, Preface.
9. *Ibid.*, Luther's Preface.
10. *The Discipline of the Methodist Church*, Par. 1585.
11. *Ibid.*
12. *The Constitution of the Presbyterian Church in the United States of America*, p. 452.
13. *The Book of Common Worship*, pp. 72, 73.
14. Eph. 4:13.

XII

1. *The Expositor's Greek Testament*, Vol. II, p. 881.
2. Simpson, P. C., *The Life of Principal Rainy*, I, 25.
3. *The Child and Religion*, edited by Thomas Stephens, pp. 278, 279.
4. *Ibid.*, p. 281.
5. *The Book of Common Prayer*.
6. Hadfield, *The Psychology of Power*, p. 50.
7. *The Book of Common Worship*, p. 64.

XIII

1. With the consent of the editor, full use has been made here of the article by the author which appeared in the summer number of *Christendom*, 1942.

Index